T0413902

CORYNNE W. PLESS
YE RIN MOK
TIM HIRSCHMANN

LOS ANGELES
INTERIORS

Lannoo

CONTENTS

02 03 04

HOLLYWOOD

EAST LOS ANGELES

WEST LOS ANGELES

INTRODUCTION

Other writers and historians have taken note of this mysterious time that Los Angeles keeps, between its past and its future. The city's abstract existence and promise of tomorrow have called the risk-takers and dreamers to its golden coasts for centuries, inviting their voices, ideas, talent, experiments, and hopes into its infinite cycle of reinvention. This daring individualism that defies time and defines this city, if this city can be defined at all, resonates within the homes and people featured in this book – illustrated through their stories of discovery and their innovative designs that speak beyond their time.

In *Los Angeles Interiors*, you'll learn how one couple got creative to win a bid for a Neutra home in Silver Lake, how a contemporary architect transformed a coastal property into a sophisticated coalescence of eras, and how one actor discovered the perfect home that observed the architectural style of the Southern city she adored but left behind for Los Angeles. Each home tells its own story and has its own unique take on design, aesthetics, and architecture, which then became difficult to categorize within one stylistic chapter. Instead, the homes are grouped geographically, loosely in and around Hollywood, the Coast, East Los Angeles, and West Los Angeles.

For those new to Los Angeles, the Hollywood landscape is as varied and bustling as the city itself. Culture is still in the making within its landmark theaters, Walk of Fame, and production lots. The Coastal homes get that warm, seaborn air through their windows at the break of day, and they are as relaxed and cool as the promising tide that surrounds them. That sought-after West Coast light also seems to have its own hue over the ocean come dusk, which in certain moments has its own spell on time. In the summer, residents of East Los Angeles hear the fireworks take to the sky from Dodger Stadium. The Los Angeles River runs dry through the valleys, except during the winter rains, and an easy hike up one of the Eastside's trails promises views of Mount Baldy, the Downtown skyline, or the Pacific on a clear day – if you're lucky. West Los Angeles's residents are perched within the area's majestic hills and canyons and get to watch the sun disappear into the Santa Monica Mountains behind them. The West also has numerous museums and is a stone's throw away from the Pacific Coast and all its greatness.

The homes featured in this book are an ode to the past, a voice of today's designs, and a nod to the future – much like the city itself, they're undefined and thriving.

Corynne W. Pless, Los Angeles

COASTAL
INTERIORS
HOLLYWOOD
EAST LOS ANGELES
WEST LOS ANGELES

01

SEA OF CHANGE

Elizabeth Paige Smith and Christopher Stringer transformed a New England-style property into the perfect coastal retreat, brimming with colorful takes on classic designs.

When Elizabeth Paige Smith and Christopher Stringer had the opportunity to create their dream home, they didn't hold back. Smith, a multidisciplinary artist, and Stringer, an industrial designer, homed in on natural materials, transitional spaces, and their intuitions to transform the four-bedroom, 1,900 sq. ft. Venice home into a creative haven that echoes their own unique, courageous tastes.

Smith compared the design journey to a bird in flight, a metaphor she artistically infused into the details of the home – specifically the center points inlaid into the wood walls and ceilings, carried out through intricate millwork. Like pelagic sunsets, these vortexes divert the gaze into a place of warmth and ease, ringing in a sense of harmony. Smith also looked to her upbringing in the Cayman Islands as a calming source of inspiration and used materials and finishes that reflect the Caribbean's mystique – like the abalone shell wall that takes over the powder room.

Organic, innovative designs continue throughout the home, where the couple reimagined their practical spaces and daily routines into engaging, one-of-a-kind experiences. In the primary bedroom, the couple built an open-concept suite, where the shower sits surrounded by glass in the center of the bedroom under a retractable skylight. Stringer then designed a custom steam snorkel that releases a billowy cloud of mist, elevating the shower experience into a spa-like dream. Additional multifunctional spaces, like the hammock hangout hallway, seashell study room, and cedar-boxed Zen room, are filled with warm, playful materials and customized furniture that speak to the calming, coastal vibes that surround the home. Smith, also a celebrated furniture designer, designed several pieces in the home, including the guest room's mahogany wood pyramid dresser, along with several unique works, like her blow tables and light-reflecting mirrors, that are sprinkled throughout.

As the couple carved into the home, they revealed original redwood tongue-and-groove ceiling boards hidden underneath layers of paint in their kitchen. They then revived

The garden window is filled with a variety of succulents. A copy of *David Hockney, A Bigger Book* is on display over the bookstand designed by Marc Newson ◄

Organic, innovative designs continue throughout the home, where the couple reimagined their practical spaces and daily routines into engaging, one-of-a-kind experiences.

→ The couple embraced the kitchen's limiting galley-like layout and installed under-counter appliances. They replaced the floors with walnut, the perfect roommate for redwood walls, and added a heating element for those chilly Pacific nights. The countertops are made of California-sourced Calacatta stone

the boards and installed a copper vessel surface lighting system between the exposed planks. As the project began to unfold, the home's warmth resonated deeply with the owners – who now end their days in a peaceful haven near the beach.

←

Within the living room's redwood plank walls, a sofa by Francesco Binfaré from Edra and a stone side table and coffee table, designed by Smith, fill the space. The artwork above the sofa was purchased in Berlin at Soul Objects. The artwork, left, is by John Baldessari. The ceiling lights are by FX Luminaire and the custom goat rugs are from Pure Rugs. The speakers, Syng Cells, were designed by Stringer to fill the space with sound

→

The custom diamond stone table displays the couple's collection of singing bowls. The green sculptural cactus was discovered in Milan and later gifted by surprise from Stringer to Smith. "I love it; it adds color and texture," says Smith

The dining room and kitchen transition naturally into the living room. Hammocks sway from the hall ceiling, and a mix of textural artworks layer the room. "It's the heart and soul of the home," says Smith

In the "seashell" room, shells and sand from Venice Beach are fastened to the wall with EcoPlaster. The wooden mahogany custom bench and drawers were designed by Smith, and the cushions were covered in a seafoam-blue mohair. The original artwork (featuring Smith) by Australia-based artist Mulga is on display next to a work by Paul McNeil. The accent silk pillows that sit over the daybed designed by Smith were picked up in a vintage shop in Australia. A vintage chess set by Carl Auböck sits above the table

A ceramic Stan Bitters pendant lights the guest room. The patterned drapery is from The Romo Group. The Pyramid dresser is made of mahogany wood, designed by Smith. The triangle mirror was sourced from Merchant Modern. The bookstand was designed by Stringer

Additional multifunctional spaces, like the hammock hangout hallway, seashell study room, and cedar-boxed Zen room, are filled with warm, playful materials that speak to the calming, coastal vibes that surround the home.

The upholstered wall
material and privacy
curtains are from
The Romo Group,
while the pyramid
dresser in
mahogany was
designed by Smith

The open suite that
sits behind the bed
was designed by
Stringer and Smith,
using Azul
Macaubas stone.
Smith's 'Infinite
Vibrations I' mirror
hangs above the
sink. The room is
dressed in cedar
walls and ceilings,
with walnut floors.

The 'DC' bed is by
Vincenzo de Cotiis
for Ceccotti, while
the crystal lighting
was designed by
Smith in
collaboration with
Robert Lewis
Lighting. Original
photographs by
Smith, part of the
Ritournelle series,
adorn the wall

A mahogany vanity with a custom California Calacatta milled sink, designed by Smith, adorns the powder room. The 'Infinite Vibrations II' mirror sculpture is a work by Smith, doubling as an everyday mirror

A Stan Bitters
pendant hangs over
the Ofuro Bathtub
by Rapsel designed
by Matteo Thun &
Antonio Rodriguez.
The framed
photographs were
taken by Smith,
part of her
Ritournelle series

CLASSICALLY ONE-OF-A-KIND

Meredith Chin brought in interior designer Mat Sanders to help her transform a dated Venice bungalow into a personal, inviting home.

For Meredith Chin, designing her first home meant telling her own story, a new visual self-discovery the filmmaker thoroughly enjoyed as a first-time homeowner. "It became a symbolic project," says Chin, whose thoughtful curation of color and furnishings naturally folded into a space where she and her guests could feel at home.

Shortly after Chin had the keys, she called on Mat Sanders, an interior designer whom she met through a mutual friend, for his ideas and expertise. "I told Mat that I just wanted a home that really looked like me. I couldn't articulate it at the time, but the more photos I pulled of things I liked, it became clearer and clearer," remembers Chin.

The home, a spacious three-bedroom bungalow in Venice with mature fruit trees and a gracious layout, had a solid foundation that gave Chin and Sanders a generous starting point. Sanders was there to help Chin translate her style through a variety of visual outlets that illustrate her own unique personality. "There are no rules for how to create such a mix; it's usually a feeling combined with some good editing.

I love vintage, so it was a significant starting point for inspiration," says Sanders.

They began with the front entryway, or lack thereof, with the front door opening straight into the living room. Chin wanted a "shoes off" household vibe, which was deemed difficult given there was no landing space or mudroom. "Creating the front entry was a key part of the design process," says Sanders. "We floated the sofa in the living room to make space for a vestibule, complete with a console table, bench, and coat hooks. This design choice ensures that guests entering through the front door don't feel like they're walking directly into a room, providing a more welcoming and functional entry experience."

Chin also wanted a living room where guests felt truly at home and could comfortably enjoy the space as much as she did. "I don't like it when a house looks really beautiful but you can't sit on anything. I wanted it to feel warm and inviting while also looking really intentional," says Chin. Chin and Sanders

A vintage reupholstered chair sits next to the living room fireplace that was framed in a simple plaster and black marble

"The color palette, mood, and aesthetic were influenced by Meredith's personal style, which featured a combination of classic elements with a modern twist," says Sanders.

brought in furniture, new and old, that exuded this personalized coziness, like the violet velvet sofa and soft white rug. They also hung works by her friends and other female artists on the customized gallery wall designed by Sanders, which elegantly displays (and conceals) the television among the collectibles and works of art.

In the kitchen, Sanders and Chin balanced the use of black with brass accents to create a classic space that is pleasing to be in. "The color palette, mood, and aesthetic were influenced by Meredith's personal style, which featured a combination of classic elements with a modern twist," says Sanders. The kitchen doors flow onto the terrace, where Chin often hosts dinner parties. "I just love how it's chic and black and so inviting," says Chin.

Within the home's mix of bold yet muted hues, beautiful custom craftsmanship, and vintage finds, you'll find an inviting, warm soul.

In the living room, the gallery wall designed by Sanders is filled with artworks by female artists and Chin's friends, including Hannah Cousins, Lauren DiCioccio, Tasha Van Zandt, Maya Rudolph, and Javier Dunn. The chair is a vintage find and sits next to a wooden bench from Lawson-Fenning

The living room walls are painted in Snowbound White. The sofa and black coffee table are from Lawson-Fenning, while the armchair is from Denmark 50 and the rug from Lawrence of La Brea

The dining room bench and chairs were designed by Thomas Hayes Studio

Stools from Thomas Hayes Studio are tucked under the kitchen island that is lit by a modern globe pendant from TRNK

"The jewel tones became a foundation for things we looked at, and it helped anchor me as we continued to build out different elements. I knew I wanted it to have art from my friends and other female artists," says Chin.

The artwork above the fluted console in the study is by Mat Sanders ←

Within the gallery wall, the pink Lady Gaga Joanne hat was a gift. Artwork by other artists featured on the wall consist of Hannah Cousins, Lauren DiCioccio, Tasha Van Zandt, Maya Rudolph, and Javier Dunn ↓

In the primary
bedroom,
the headboard,
designed by Sanders,
features a floating
pillow board fastened
to a brass bar.
The wainscoting was
painted in Tarrytown
Green. An 'Alta'
brass dome from
Lawson-Fenning
lights the room, while
French doors open
to a side terrace

The bathroom's relaxing aesthetic consists of black-trimmed windows, serene white floors (and walls), mid-century lighting, and golden faucets

COASTAL

NEW ENDEAVORS

Sandrine Abessera and Lubov Azria worked to create a home that would honor the architect's minimalist design and suit their newest venture – a residential salon.

"We entered the house and couldn't stop thinking about it," remembers Sandrine Abessera, recalling the moments after she and Lubov Azria toured a listing they discovered online.

Designed by minimalist architect Kurt Simon, the three-bedroom, three-story home was built in the 1980s and overlooks the Venice Canal. The home's magnetic charm begins at its entry, where a narrow stairwell takes you up into the living room's 27-foot-tall ceilings. The bright yet intimate quarters boast views of the romantic canal through their floor-to-ceiling windows. The abundance of natural light, gracious layout, epic views, and architectural history won over Azria and Abessera instantly. "We fell in love with the space," says Abessera.

Abessera, an artist, and Azria, also an artist and former chief creative officer of BCBG Max Azria, quickly realized the house was more than just a home. The blank canvas-like aesthetic, with tall white walls and an open floor plan, sparked the idea of a residential salon, a place where artists, designers, and creatives could exhibit new works and ideas. They named the venture Maison Lune, then quickly met with curators and reached out to friends to help manage the salon's inauguration and initial growth. "Right away the space had the energy of sharing talents," remembers Azria.

When it came to the home's core design, they pulled together an intimate list of designers and artists to help furnish the space in a unified aesthetic that would pair effortlessly with rotating works. They found Gabriella Kuti, who stepped in to oversee the home's interior design. At Zona Maco, Mexico City's annual art and furniture fair, Abessera and Azria met Alexander Díaz Andersson of Atra furniture. They were deeply drawn to his designs and commissioned several sets and custom pieces that would fill each story and work cohesively in altered environments. Rugs were brought in by Henzel Studio from Sweden, with a few of the bathroom wall sconces designed by Amande Haeghen. They partnered with a local store, Merit, which brings in temporary vintage finds to fill the spaces as they change, like the stackable Willy Guhl shelving seen in the kitchen.

In the primary bedroom, a pair of wooden works from South Africa are displayed under artwork by Santiago Martínez Peral

37

The unconventional yet vogue approach to exhibiting art in their personal space is an opportunity that Abessera and Azria feel overwhelmingly grateful for. "It's amazing to live with the artist's energy," says Abessera.

The cohesive yet simple mix of one-of-a-kind pieces came together just in time for Maison Lune's first exhibition, *Transcendence,* curated by Gaïa Jacquet-Matisse, in the fall of 2022. The unconventional yet vogue approach to exhibiting art in their personal space is an opportunity that Abessera and Azria feel overwhelmingly grateful for. "It's amazing to live with the artist's energy," says Abessera.

When Abessera and Azria are not working on Maison Lune, they are living in it. The kitchen, with its views of the canal, lower ceilings, big island, and overall cozy feel, is a favorite spot in the home. When guests and friends are over, they also congregate in the space. The primary bedroom's expansive layout hosts a spacious living area, jet pool, and workspace. The upstairs guest room showcases more works, mostly in their permanent collection. The home's many levels continue in the same visual breath, where inspiration lies in every corner. All in all, Abessera and Azria have thoughtfully orchestrated a beautiful new chapter of the home that honors the architect's legacy.

The living room's sectional, designed by Atra, is made of alpaca. The shelf was customized to hold additional artworks on a smaller scale. Artworks by Bobbie Oliver (left) and Edson Fernandes (right), grace the walls. The chairs and coffee table are also by Atra

The primary bedroom, located on the first floor, has a spacious sitting area where more temporary and permanent works are on display. The Atra-designed armchairs and daybed fill the space, delineated by Henzel rugs. Artworks by Santiago Martínez Peral hang on the walls

The Noguchi lamps were original to the home when they bought it and currently light the dining room table and chairs, designed by Atra. Artwork by Edson Fernandes hangs next to the stairs, while vessels by Natalya Seva adorn the table

The 'Sponeck' patio furniture is by Iota, while the wooden dining table set was designed by Atra

The home's many levels continue
in the same visual breath, where
inspiration lies in every corner.

A small jet pool sits off the primary bedroom's small office, where
Azria works. A mix of vintage pieces collected by Abessera and Azria,
like the South African stools, mingle with contemporary works, like
the Karakter Aldo Bakker console ←

The home's entrance begins at the stairwell below the living room. The ↓
wall's recessed shelf was added to accommodate additional smaller
works of art to display

↑

More artworks by
Santiago Martínez
Peral hang over
Azria's permanent
collection of
sculptures by Hanns-
Peter Krafft

The wall sconces
designed by Amande
Haeghen add a bit
of fluidity to
the bathroom,
complementing the
earthy black-and-
white marble accents

ODE TO THE PAST

David Kitz and Kate Brien Kitz collaborated with architect Andrew Hall, who took their cultivated aspirations and the practical necessities of a growing family and designed a one-of-a-kind architectural gem that harkens back to design's best of times.

It all began in a friend's kitchen. Kate Brien Kitz, a fashion stylist, and David Kitz, a photographer, were dipping into parenthood and home buying at the same time. They wanted their new home, a three-bedroom bungalow in Mar Vista, to speak to their own individuality and nod to the historic architects they long admired, all while keeping the home's original Japanese-style facets intact – and, well, they weren't sure where to start.

Kate and David were soon introduced to Andrew Hall, of Aha Design, their mutual friend's kitchen's architect, who was just stepping out on his own after a seasoned tenure at an established architecture firm. Hall was quick to pick up the project's scope and potential. "It was clear that the former owners had loved the place and put a lot of effort and energy into making it their own, and Kate and David saw that," says Hall. That sense of virtue and longevity was then woven into the home's next chapter, where Hall inlaid, through intricate detailing, a lasting impression of novel architectural designs that spoke to the couple's refined style and the habits of a budding family.

Before they broke ground, the couple and Hall laid it all out, agreeing first that those original charming facets, such as the wood detailing, Dutch gable roof, stone fireplace, and Japanese ceiling light, were all there to stay. During their initial meetings, the couple pulled from their colorful library the bookmarked pages from Alvar Aalto books, among other designers, to reference. "It was very collaborative with Kate and David. They were incredibly savvy and capable at reading and navigating the architectural, visual communication," says Hall. "They came to the table with a lot of ideas and a very tight material palette."

The new parents chose sturdy materials (like wood, concrete, and drywall) that would survive through the fads and inevitable wear and tear. "We wanted it to feel timeless to a certain degree. We didn't want it to feel overly trendy. We didn't want it to feel like we were making stylistic decisions that five to ten years down the line, we'd look at and go 'Oh, that was very 2020,'" says David, "We wanted it to feel like we were pulling

On the front porch, evenly spaced vertical planks of wood act as a soft boundary between the interior of the home and the sidewalk. A "nice telescopic moment of the house," Hall adds

from the best of midcentury." Hall found creative ways to express their combined ideas through large- and small-scale structural designs, seen through the home's expansion and the crafted millwork that defines the cabinetry, storage benches, and custom furniture pieces sprinkled throughout. "[Andrew's] attention to details is just incredible, and he's so thoughtful," says Kate.

Hall delicately revised the existing floor plan, adding more space and specific customized built-ins that enlightened the couple to envision the property's full potential. "One of the benefits of working with an existing building is the limitations it gives you also afford the opportunity to do something more interesting and more tailored in terms of a new space," says Hall. To start, Hall included a two-story addition off the back of the home, topping it with a matching Dutch gable roof, which provided the couple with a more spacious primary bedroom, bathroom, and closet, and a new family room tucked underneath.

He brought in the ground floor's square ceramic tiles, customized wood furnishings, datum shelves, and textured glass panes in order to help unify new and old. He then added a new living room off the existing dining room, where the home once ended, and placed a slight grade change between the two rooms. He embraced this moment vertically as well, raising the ceiling height a few feet and adding a skylight. This simple play with space and light gave the couple a stately yet casual living room with phenomenal views into their backyard and of the clouds and sun that hold it all together.

The corner of this new living room is flanked by a sea of windows with integrated screens, a nod to the rice paper screens that were once in the home, and a customized wooden sectional adhered to the wall. The anchored sofa is snuggled into the corner, where Hall finds the most interesting architecture is happening. "It's where the gardens, light, and air are flowing the best," adds Hall. Kate and David also worked with Lafayette Studio, who advised the couple on a few of the floating furniture pieces and fabrics that now fill and speak to the space. "The house feels like everything in it is really meaningful to us," says Kate.

When it came to the lawn, the couple wanted to privatize the yard and create a natural, safe escape into the fresh air. "We knew what we wanted in a sense but did not have the tools to put it into fruition," says Kate. Kate and David were introduced to Molly Funk, Mary Lange, and Donielle Kaufman, who brought their dreams of an adventurous, secluded backyard to life. Pollinator-friendly plants, and lots of them, were planted into the more "wabi sabi" outdoor design, a desired contender to the more linear angles within the walls. "It really felt like a renaissance, like a new beginning for us. It felt like we could really build memories and essentially begin our family in this home," says David.

The second story is accessed through the sculptural staircase. A skylight lights the space ←

←

A work by Paul Jenkins that once belonged to Kate's grandfather hangs in the living room next to a Brendan Ravenhill sconce. The accent panels and structural beams are made of Douglas Fir. "I like [Douglas Fir's] versatility in it being a structural material and a finish material," says Hall. Vintage nesting stools from Amsterdam Modern and a pair of vintage Ikea wooden chairs offer additional seating. The sectional is covered in a soft, white fabric from Holly Hunt

→

The original fireplace and Japanese ceiling light bring a sense of warmth and texture to the dining room. Vintage 'Cesca' chairs designed by Marcel Breuer surround a custom glass table

Pendants from In Common With light the kitchen, while vintage Charlotte Perriand counter stools are tucked under the Taj Mahal Quartzite countertops from Stoneland USA. Heath tiles in Chamois form the kitchen's backsplash

"One of the benefits of working with an existing building is the limitations it gives you also afford the opportunity to do something more interesting and more tailored in terms of a new space," says Hall.

Outside the living room's sea of windows, the pollinators are buzzing and the coastal light casts its silhouettes within ←

A Queensland bottle tree grabs light through the skylight above the exposed and inlaid Douglas Fir structural beams. An Isamu Noguchi pendant brings additional light to the landing ↓

→

The primary bedroom's linens are from Parachute and layered with a Coyuchi blanket. A Lars Elkind painting, created in 1964, hangs over the bedside table. The custom recessed sofa designed by Hall gives the parents an additional place to relax and read with their kids

The bathroom
features walls and
floors clad in almond
Daltile tiles and
custom cabinetry
in Douglas Fir

COASTAL
HOLLYWOOD
INTERIORS
EAST LOS ANGELES
WEST LOS ANGELES

02

CALIFORNIA DREAM

Sophie Lawrence Parker and Kevin Parker partnered with Jaime Lee Major to fill their new Los Angeles hillside home with nothing but color.

Sophie Lawrence Parker, an entrepreneur, and musician Kevin Parker, of Tame Impala, are both originally from Australia, but nearly five years ago, they acted on the budding thought of making Los Angeles a home away from home. "It was kind of like a Los Angeles test to see if we enjoyed living there," remembers Sophie. It didn't take long for the city to serenade them with its natural surroundings and historical makeup, and they soon began looking for a place to call home. Their agent called with a home to tour, warning it was nothing they wanted – meaning it lacked a pool or anything resembling midcentury. But the home's Spanish-style architecture boasted arched windows with breathtaking views of the city and had an unspoken warmth that inevitably pulled them in.

After months of living in the home with minimal furnishings, beanbags included, Sophie began to look for help. She was soon introduced to Jaime Lee Major, of Major Spaces, a designer who recently stepped away from a career in fashion and into the interiors world. Over brunch, they discussed the potential project, shared their love of bold color in whimsical designs, and relished in the fact that they were all from the same small town in Australia – basically sealing the deal.

Since the couple travels often, splitting their downtime between Australia and Los Angeles, it was important that the space felt calm, but it also had to be fun. "Stimulating calmness" is how Sophie described the aesthetic goal, which Major then hemmed in beautifully. Major proposed vibrant colors, customized furniture, and swooning designer pieces to create an interesting dialogue that didn't overwhelm. "They wanted to to keep the walls white but bring in lots of color," remembers Major.

For color inspiration, Sophie often referenced the childhood movie she and Kevin were fond of, the original 1970s *Willy Wonka & the Chocolate Factory*. The film's spectrum of deep lilacs, translucent jades, sky blues, and golden tangerines were kept as a back-pocket palette of sorts and sprinkled throughout. Major often took over rooms in a full monochromatic

The recessed arched shelf, ornate tiles, and wrought iron railing were all original to the home

Rolling hillside views surround the century-old home.

scheme, like the light-blue dressing room and lilac breakfast nook. Each room taps a sort of curiosity that ushers you in, like a magical, prismatic tide.

When it came to the furniture, the beanbags were gone but not forgotten, and the couple brought in other beloved pieces that exuded comfort and were resilient to fads. The living room's midcentury sofa was reupholstered in sunny chartreuse, alongside the set of vintage Mario Bellini chairs reupholstered in warm coral. Major recognized that the furniture and designs in the inspiration images she and Sophie often shared had curvy tendencies. An amoeba-shaped wooden coffee table, custom headboard in velvet lilac, and vintage Ettore Sottsass mirror all reflect the playful, fluid movements Sophie and Major both adored. A vintage Mickey Mouse dresser, found on 1st Dibs, was put in the nursery. They then honed in on the dresser's retro vibe, bringing in the yellow Entler Studio light and wavy rainbow rug. "I love fun, fantastical kinds of things, and there's no place better than a kid's room to scratch that itch," says Sophie.

The home's colorful personality, subtle surprises, and playful elements glow from room to room. "The house is so stimulating to me, like Los Angeles is. I love being there," says Sophie.

→ The kitchen was a perfect space that they didn't want to touch. It boasts ornate original Spanish tile and a window that overlooks the Hollywood sign

Each room taps a sort of
curiosity that ushers you in,
like a magical, prismatic tide.

The artwork in the living room is by John Prince Siddon, a Western   ← ←
Australian First Nations artist. "Finding a painting that fit that space, that
was also a reference to our home, was amazing," says Sophie. They then
outfitted the furniture colors and fabrics to work cohesively with
the painting. The rug is by Christopher Farr and part of a Studio
Shamshiri collaboration

The dry bar was customized by Major. "This is my favorite thing in the whole   ←
house," says Sophie. The table and chairs were a Danish 1960s set

"I love fun interpretations of normal, everyday things you use," says   ↓
Sophie, whose unique collection of pieces picked up from here and there fill
the shelves in their breakfast nook

A vintage sofa recovered in a sunny chartreuse sits over a rug by Christopher Farr, part of a Studio Shamshiri collaboration

A vintage sculpture piece and mirror were found online at a shop in Los Angeles. The Italian art deco ceiling light was found on 1st Dibs. The light's glass is tinted in a mint green, something they adored, working the color into other areas in the room. Vintage burl wood bedside tables sit next to the custom bed, layered in Missoni fabrics

The room's color was inspired from the Entler ceiling light. The room's nod to surrealism is something Sophie admires and finds soothing. "It feels like you're in the sky," says Sophie

The Mickey Mouse
mini-dresser was the
first piece that came
into the room. Major
then built the room
around it. The wavy
wool rug is from
Design Within
Reach; the light is
by Entler Studio

FOREVER HOLLYWOOD

Kimberly Biehl Boaz and Greg Boaz filled Mae West's former apartment with everything West, everything Boaz, and lots of Hollywood.

Kimberly Biehl Boaz's path into Mae West's former apartment started with cocktails at Musso & Frank. There, a friend of Kimberly's, who also shared a deep enthusiasm for all things Old Hollywood, told her he had just toured the screen legend's former apartment, which was now for rent. Kimberly wasted no time in contacting the manager, and within 15 minutes of touring the space, she knew it had to be hers.

Kimberly, an interior designer, along with her husband Greg Boaz, a musician, thoughtfully brought in historical pieces and heirlooms that reflect their own personal tastes but also nod to the life and times of West, one of Hollywood's most controversial and glamorous stars of her time.

Once word got out about Kimberly's exciting move, the calls and texts from friends and colleagues requesting an invitation never ended. Kimberly decided to host an all-weekend party and had friends pick a day and time to drop by, but it didn't stop there. Eventually the space took on a life of its own, and Kimberly and Greg found themselves hosting regular salons, and at times themed parties, with new and old acquaintances wanting in. Their guest book is filled with signatures from friends, actors, producers, and Hollywood enthusiasts – including a few cartoons by Disney illustrators. "So many friendships have been born here. It has turned into a very cool part of our lives. We didn't expect it to be that," says Kimberly.

When it came to decorating, Kimberly went for a 1930s Parisian art nouveau theme that mixed moody hues, subtle glitz, patterned textures, and, of course, bits of Mae West. Kimberly, who began trawling through estate sales, auctions, and garage sales at the age of 16, pulled from her large inventory of one-of-kind pieces to fill the home's many corners. The bookshelf reflected in the living room's mirror belonged to Elizabeth Taylor and Richard Burton and came from the actors' Mexico estate, serendipitously called Casa Kimberly – a must-have, Kimberly admits. Kimberly's parents gifted her with the original West family crest, which was rehung in the exact place it hung back in 1932.

In the living room, a Cole Porter portrait by artist Jirayr Zorthian sits above a carved lion chair, reupholstered in olive mohair. The sculpture on the side table is by local artist Pat Berger

When it came to decorating, Kimberly went for a 1930s Parisian art nouveau theme that mixed moody hues, subtle glitz, patterned textures, and, of course, bits of Mae West.

← Lined with portraits, the living room wall features 1930s sconces from the original El Royale apartment building in LA's Hancock Park. The barrel tables, purchased at auction, belonged to actor Mary Pickford, while the chesterfield sofa is from Restoration Hardware

In the living room, painted portraits discovered at auctions, random garage sales, and the occasional alley, adorn the walls. Kimberly has even had guests help identify some of the unknown subjects, like the Robert Ryan portrait that hangs near other acts like Grayson Hall and Luise Rainer. Kimberly covered the room's existing buttery-white walls in a warm, caramel-hued wallpaper and replaced the window's white mini-blinds with deep, moody drapes, circling back to that Parisian flair.

→ Acting as a headboard in the primary bedroom is a four-panel screen discovered on Craigslist, which Kimberly guesses dates from the 1960s

The bathroom's 1930s tiles were original to the building, along with a few of the chandeliers. The neon sign was picked up from the Seymour Stein estate sale. The tiles, in great condition, speak to the other tenants, who, like Kimberly, were careful (and honored) to keep the home in its best condition. "Everyone who has moved in were fans of Mae's," adds Kimberly.

"So many friendships have been born here. It has turned into a very cool part of our lives. We didn't expect it to be that," says Kimberly.

The wallpaper by Nina Campbell for Osborne & Little brings a bit of the Parisian salon aesthetic to the dining room. The chandelier, original to the apartment, is repeated throughout the home. The pair of red lacquer chairs belonged to Mary Pickford ←

The lamp, previously belonging to Ozzy Osbourne, sits next to Biehl's great-grandfather's Marxophone and small ceramic works that belonged to James Garner ↓

The lilac bathroom
tiles were original
to the apartment.
The neon sign was
picked up from the
Seymour Stein
estate sale

On the top shelf sits
a Bob Baker
Marionette original
carving of Pinocchio
for Walt Disney and
a work by Biehl's
daughter. Moving
down, Mae West's
shoes and
accessories sit next
to a pair of John
Lennon's glasses
above a few of Cary
Grant's books.
Additional items
include West's rent
check, James
Garner's shaving kit,
Rose Marie's SAG
card, and Biehl's
lucky penny box full
of pennies, among
many others

BALANCING ACT

Rosa Park and Rich Stapleton's admiration and respect for owning a century-old home guided how they creatively carved in their own imprint.

As Rosa Park and Rich Stapleton prepared for their transatlantic move from Europe to Los Angeles, finding the perfect home to put down roots was crucial. After what felt like the search that never ended, they finally found "the one," a Spanish-Colonial two-story home with private gardens, secluded guest quarters, and original twentieth century architectural detailing. Park, co-founder of *Cereal* Magazine and director and founder of Francis Gallery, and Stapleton, a photographer, have a sensibility for art and design that is beautifully reflected in their practices and personal collections. The couple reveled in the opportunity to own a century-old home and planned a renovation that perfectly balances preservation and contemporary living. "I do think the best preserving arises from maintaining the integrity of something and still making it relevant to the time you live in," says Park.

They began with the given layout and kept the renovations simple, non-structural, and purely decorative. "It was more altering the design decisions that the previous owners had made, which just weren't aligned to ours. So kind of respectfully doing as little work as possible while still making the house feel like our home," says Park, "... and that takes time." Park removed the more flourished details, like the glass chandeliers and glossy hardware, and introduced a softer atmosphere using a simple color palette with rustic finishes to complement their own earthy, soothing aesthetics.

As they moved in, the new home came with a few learning curves as well, including designing with their new son in mind – a first for the couple. "Beforehand, we decorated just for us," says Park, who embraced the new challenge of merging her favorite designs into a space that needed to be practical, safe, and comfortable – an art in and of itself. "It was that nurture of what I love, but trying to make it also family friendly," says Park. She pulled in low pieces for softer landings, like the Mario Bellini sofa in the living room, and swapped out the kitchen's existing marble floor for wood. Park also applied soft, deep shades of green to

A gold leaf painting purchased from Mjölk hangs above a vintage Spanish dresser in the primary bedroom. The earth-red sculpture is by Minjae Kim

"I do think the best preserving arises from maintaining the integrity of something and still making it relevant to the time you live in," says Park.

several rooms to reflect the peaceful, grassy hills of England – a comfort she came to miss after the move.

The home's best-kept secret is the siloed top floor, where the couple hosts visiting friends, family, and gallery artists. "My husband and I knew we'd be hosting a lot of friends," says Park. "It's the ideal setup for hosting guests long term because they have complete privacy," she adds. Guests can access the stairs through the entrance and enjoy an entire second floor (identical to the ground-floor layout), with their own kitchen, living room, and bedrooms. When guests are not in town, the couple prefers the upstairs dining room to host dinner parties and gatherings. "It has this very peaceful view of the rooftops of the neighborhood houses and palm trees, and the sunrise and sunsets are so special because the light fills into that room," adds Park.

As Park and Stapleton continue to observe their own patterns in the home, they fearlessly fold new ideas and works of art into the spaces – an ever-changing scheme with new developments on the horizon.

→ In the living room, an Isamu Noguchi floor lamp lights the corner of the living room, next to the wooden chair by Minjae Kim. The art deco sconce is original to the home

The home's best-kept secret
is the siloed top floor, where
the couple hosts visiting friends,
family, and gallery artists.

An Isamu Noguchi light sits in the corner of the living
room. The couch, by Mario Bellini for B&B Italia, is
complemented by an Armadillo rug, a chair designed by
artist Minjae Kim, and an artwork (right) by Liam
Stevens. The 1920s sconce is original to the home

An Isamu Noguchi pendant lights the upstairs dining
room. An artwork by John Zabawa hangs on the wall,
while chairs by George Nakashima and a table by
Danielle Siggerud for Audo take center stage

The soft Mario Belleni sofa sits next to a 'Moon' jar
gifted by artist Nancy Kwon

The kitchen's custom countertops are made out of walnut and white marble

In the upstair's
hallway, an art deco
pendant original to
the home lights the
space leading into
the dining room

In the primary bedroom, one of two white lamps from Mary MacGill in Germantown, New York, sits above the wooden nightstand

The bathroom's
deep-green hue was
chosen to reflect the
lush hills of England.
The vanity is made
of an elegant marble
and golden faucets

LACONIC GRANDEUR

A grand estate was revived and restored by The Future Perfect's David Alhadeff, who thoughtfully brought the home back to its original glory.

When David Alhadeff came across a vast, 7,000 sq. ft. estate for sale online, he was intrigued, very intrigued, but ultimately he passed. Alhadeff, founder of The Future Perfect, a design gallery with prestigious curatorial exhibits in several locations across North American coasts, was looking for the gallery's next outpost, as well as a place to call home. As the estate quietly sat on the market, Alhadeff's agent suggested a visit, which he remembers begrudgingly agreeing to. But once Alhadeff entered the property, he was captivated. "I rode through the gate and it was a jaw-dropping experience," recalls Alhadeff.

Designed by architect Arthur S. Heineman in 1916, the property was once notably home to movie producer Samuel Goldwyn (along with a few other famous families and guests who were whispered to Alhadeff by his new neighbors). "There were all of these beautiful architectural details. It's over 100 years old," says Alhadeff. The home's original accents, boundless gardens, and grand entertaining rooms welcomed endless work and play opportunities for

Alhadeff, his husband Jason Duzansky, and their son Leo. "I was charmed," remembers Alhadeff.

In order to fully realize the property's potential, the couple started by noting and preserving the home's original assets, like the round-arched windows and detailed moldings. "We wanted to cosmetically bring it back to its original grandeur," says Alhadeff.

Alhadeff captained the search for new materials, textures, and finishes that embodied an elegant patina. The terracotta floor was replaced with marble, stone was brought in from a seventeenth century chateau, and the walls were refinished in an opulent, weathered look – all reflecting the timeless elegance the home was meant for. To revive the plaster walls, the couple selected Kamp Studios, who added charming touches throughout, including the ribbed plaster in the main hall. The less glamorous details were also addressed, like the stripping of 300 recessed lighting

In the hallway, Eric Roinestad's V227 sculpture balances on the natural oak Noga table by Christian Woo. The glass sculpture 'Sine' is by John Hogan

"We wanted to cosmetically bring it back to its original grandeur," says Alhadeff.

→ A 'Flora' chandelier by Sophie Lou Jacobsen for In Common With complements the lounge area's classical floral frieze, while an abstract painting by Adja Yunkers bring a contemporary edge. The Sidekicks Coffee Table and Belle Reeve Sofa are by De La Espada. The ceramic sculptures, 'Tall Oblique Variation Vessel 3' and 'Small Octahedron Vessel 11', are by Cody Hoyt

fixtures and the replacement of the paper-covered wiring. "We took out a lot of the 1990s," says Alhadeff.

When it came to the garden, Alhadeff admits it was a learning curve. The couple worked with Studio Art Luna, who brought their dreams of an artful but practical outdoor escape to life.

Alhadeff discovered quickly how the juxtaposition of The Future Perfect's varying contemporary styles and the home's classical dispositions pushes guests to engage in a deeper way. "It creates a moment of 'wow.' You expect one thing, and it's serving up something very different," says Alhadeff.

These experimental and daring design philosophies are also reflected in artworks curated around the home, in both the permanent collections and rotating exhibitions. Engaging sculptural works by Karl Zahn light the foyer, where one-of-a-kind pieces, including a blown-glass coffee table by John Hogan and dining chairs by Chris Wolston, take center stage.

Throughout the space, Alhadeff's curations spark an interesting dialogue. He has elegantly authored an alternative way for his family – and anyone who enters the gallery – to view, enjoy, and revel in great design.

Each room is elegantly layered in simple, daring designs by various artists and designers.

The foyer's pilasters and plaster were thoughtfully restored by Kamp Studios and form the perfect backdrop to a selection of organic designs, including Karl Zahn 'Stratus' sconces and a 'Blume' coffee table by John Hogan for The Future Perfect. Additionally, a Chris Wolston Oro Chair, Ian Collings' 'Stone Object 09', and 'Butter', 'Array', and 'Blushy Disk' glass sculptures by John Hogan adorn the room

Under the Karl Zahn 'Stratus 07.01' chandelier, the wooden dining table by Yabu Pushelberg for Collection Particulière hosts beautiful evenings with the couple's family, friends, designers, artists, and guests. The dining room walls are covered in 'Wanderlust' by Calico. Group cocktail chairs by Philippe Malouin for SCP and glassware by Alexander Kirkeby surround the table

In the hallway, a white glass 'Bauer' chandelier by Jason Miller for Roll & Hill is suspended over checkered floor tiles by Ancient Surfaces. The ribbed plaster detail seen on the walls was done by Kamp Studios. Chris Wolston's 'Hand' Chandelier is hung in the background near an Arflex Strips sofa system, a plaster sculpture, 'Untitled 2021', by Guy Corriero, and Ben Barber's 'Xenolith' Table

←

The bedroom's drapes by Kiva Motnyk hang next to the 'Carlton' bed by Jason Miller for De La Espada and Autumn Casey's 'The Grapes' lamp. The 'Rodin' sconces and bedside tables are all by Rhode Island–based designers Ben & Aja Blanc. The 'Flora' wallpaper in Lavender is by Lindsey Adelman for Calico

→

The Rough dining table by Collection Particulière displays several Cody Hoyt ceramics ('Tall Oblique Variation Vessel 3', 'Small Octahedron Vessel 11', 'Tall Twisted Box', 'Large Oblique Vessel 1'). The Pia dining chair by Collection Particulière adds a bit texture and warmth to the space

An Eric Roinestad
vase holds fresh
flowers in the pink-
and-black tiled
bathroom

LAYERED ELEGANCE

A two-story home overlooking a private lake in Los Angeles is not an everyday find. Annie Potts and James Hayman jumped at the opportunity to live lakeside and worked to transform the property into the perfect dwelling for the couple and their family.

Annie Potts spent the last few years reimagining her Toluca Lake house into the creatively bold and inviting home that it has become, a true reflection of the actor herself. Its New Orleans–style architecture, plus its breathtaking views of the lake, made it a kismet find for Potts and her husband, James Hayman, who had recently returned to Los Angeles from New Orleans for work. Potts redesigned each room to perfectly host her family and their sterling collection of art, furniture, and heirlooms. The home's interior style and influence are credited to the Crescent City's unique design personality that celebrates French traditionalism with modern twists, while also emphasizing, in true New Orleans fashion, that anything goes.

Upon entering the home, the front door opens into the foyer, and a faux-zebra rug guides guests into the stairwell and formal sitting room, which boasts a medley of cherished pieces collected by the couple over the years. The pink chaise has been with Potts for nearly 45 years and was recently recovered in a 'Tigre' print by Scalamandré. The room's

modern furnishings layered in soft textures and bright kilims emanate a warmth that flows throughout the home.

The dining room opens to the patio and kitchen. The dining table was bequeathed to Potts by her good friend Emily Levin. "A lot of wonderful, great minds and writers sat around that table," says Potts. "It's got a certain magic to it." Potts found the landscape painting by Ralph Quackenbush at a pop-up gallery in Santa Barbara over her son's wedding weekend. "Every piece of art that I have has a story," says Potts, who has audaciously sourced paintings from local antique shops, galleries, and the deep pages of eBay.

The family room reaches out to the patio, where the pool and breathtaking views of the lake await. Vintage scores like the orange sectional from the 1960s and an illuminated diver girl from a secondhand store bring color and story to the space.

When it came to the kitchen, Potts and Hayman went for a complete renovation. The original floor level sat 18 inches above the ground floor, which closed in the height to a degree

A glamorous three-tiered golden chandelier from Currey & Company hangs below the living area's vaulted ceiling

The home's interior style and influence are credited to the Crescent City's unique design personality that celebrates French traditionalism with modern twists.

that Potts and Hayman felt was unnecessary. As they began to peel away, they discovered a yellow 1960s linoleum tile underneath, which was replaced with a beautiful, honey-toned hardwood. The kitchen was quickly set for great heights, and Potts designed a functional, stylish space, outfitted in all new appliances and custom storage. "I cook a lot, so I needed it to be functional," says Potts.

When Potts was in her twenties, she bought her first home accessory, a thin, vertical mirror, for $12. She found a durable frame and has kept it with her ever since. The mirror, now surrounded by the soft-pink Gucci 'Heron' wallpaper, floats above the powder room sink, with golden accessories adding to the room's dreamy curation.

The primary bedroom's painting was gifted to Potts from a friend, who found it in her basement. Potts was unable to identify the artist but discovered the work is a depiction of one of Pablo Picasso's costumes designed for Sergei Diaghilev's Ballets Russes. "It has all kinds of excellent history," says Potts. The work now hangs above the bed and was given an ornate golden frame. Potts has brought the painting's soft hues of mint and rose, surrounded by a touch of gold, delicately within the rest of the room's furnishings and accessories.

The home's harmonious design rhythms and spontaneous touches continue to the exterior, where Potts and Hayman can look out over the lake, dine with guests, or go for a boat ride. "We're outside a lot," says Potts. "It's so lovely."

➤ A pair of Tibetan cabinets found in Santa Fe are cherished pieces that lived another life as an extra-long sideboard in the kitchen of Potts' previous home, a Spanish hacienda in Tarzana. The artwork is by Ralph Quackenbush

110

"Every piece of art that I have has a story," says Potts, who has audaciously sourced paintings from local antique shops, galleries, and the deep pages of eBay.

The fiddle leaf fig tree fills the corner of the family room that opens to the patio overlooking the lake. A moroccan rug from Etsy and a vintage sofa from Sunbeam Vintage bring color and texture into the space

The white-coated 'Agnes' pendant, by AERIN from Visual Comfort & Co, subtly brings shape and light into the primary bedroom. The wall color is Swiss Coffee by Dunn Edwards

The elegant bathroom consists of white tile, living brass faucets (that patina with age), and a black marble tub. The portrait is of Potts' great grandmother, Hattie Harris, and was painted by Ann Baskerville in 1963

The zebra rug in the foyer was found online. An array of framed photographs and artwork fill the walls. The golden statue is of Buddha

In the guest powder room, Potts found a pale-pink Gucci 'Heron' wallpaper with a golden sea fan pendant purchased in New Orleans

THE HAILEY HOUSE

A Neutra home perched in the Hollywood hills was brought back to its original greatness through the thought and care of chief creative officer Patrick Thomas O'Neill.

Patrick Thomas O'Neill's discovery and admiration of midcentury architecture began while watching the film *The Ice Storm*, a 1997 drama directed by Ang Lee. The striking yet sophisticated interiors from the film's cast of minimalist-style homes resonated so deeply with O'Neill that he decided to build his own modernist retreat (with the help of architect Audrey Matlock) in the Catskills, just a few years following the film's debut. After ten years or so of enjoying his own modernist escape, it came time for the bicoastal chief creative officer to exchange his beloved home for a more permanent tenure in California. O'Neill's personal experience with architecture's ability to inspire and enlighten (coupled with his California upbringing, where the buildings by Craig Ellwood and Frank Gehry were just a detour away) made the news of a Richard Neutra pocket listing in the Hollywood Hills a must-see.

Perhaps it was the quietened real estate market in 2012, the distraction of the holidays, or O'Neill's hastened offer after touring the historic property (or all of the above), but come the New Year, and much to his surprise, O'Neill

became the fourth owner of Richard Neutra's Hailey House. The home, named after its original owner, was built in 1959 and tucked into one of Hollywood's lush hillsides. The 1,200 sq. ft. layout hosts one bedroom and two bathrooms, modular social areas, and a deck overlooking the city's romantic skyline.

The home was left mostly untouched by the previous owners, but O'Neill wanted to remove even the minimal interventions and bring it back to its true, original state. "I decided when I got it, I wanted to restore the house to the original vision of Richard Neutra, color scheme and everything," says O'Neill. O'Neill then called Dr. Barbara Lamprecht, who became the property's project manager. "Having her by my side was critical," says O'Neill. Lamprecht discovered the home's original plans and specs from the archives, which the two then referenced closely. Lamprecht also pulled in skilled subcontractors who understood Neutra's vision and the fragility and importance of its renovation. O'Neill also found the original color palette suggested by

A Swedish bronze light sculpture by Tom Ahlstrom & Hans Ehrlich is on display over the fireplace and the Gilbert Rohde coffee table. The framed screenprint is by Andy Warhol

"I decided when I got it, I wanted to restore the house to the original vision of Richard Neutra, color scheme and everything," says O'Neill.

Neutra (including the current interior walls' persimmon and the exterior's muted yellow) and even located the same American Standard bathroom faucets in backstock in Pasadena, all in their original packaging. "Neutra had an artist's sensibility; I think that's what I'm responding to. There was an appreciation of details that you didn't necessarily see that went through the whole experience of the homeowner," says O'Neill. "I just brought it all back to what he wanted."

When it came to furnishing the space, O'Neill collaborated with artist and interior designer Anthony Barsoumian. The two creatives brought in an assortment of art and furniture from a range of eras. "I tried to grab from different countries and different influences and mix it up a little bit," says O'Neill. In the family room, a 1958 Eames speaker, when it's not in use, doubles as a side table. In the living room, you'll find a black Milo Baughman calfskin chair from the 1950s, a Gilbert Rohde coffee table from the 1940s, and De Sede leather patchwork ottoman from the 1970s. "I do like to be reminded of things that somewhat took a lot of time to think about and design. There are different eras and different countries, so appreciating this sort of global midcentury things," adds O'Neill.

The glass walls and windows that look out onto the home's serene surroundings provide that sought-after illusive connection to the outside. "It was a huge move to bring [the outdoors] in; it represented the future and future way of living. That optimism, I'm really attracted to," says O'Neill. "It was really more about the new way of living, a better way of living for everyone."

→ In the kitchen, O'Neill touched up a few of the wall cabinets with smoke-screen glass sliding doors with mirrors adhered to the back to "feel more sophisticated and add more space"

"Neutra had an artist's sensibility; I think that's what I'm responding to. There was an appreciation of details that you didn't necessarily see that went through the whole experience of the homeowner," says O'Neill.

O'Neill softened the feel of the living room by removing the paper accordion modular wall and attaching white curtains to the partition's hardware. The two-tier brass and black glass DIA coffee table is next to Vladimir Kagan's 'Swanback' sofa. The television is displaying a screen saver by Clare E. Rojas. Surrounding the television (counterclockwise) is a watercolor by Carl Hopgood and a portrait of Carl Hopgood by Johnnie Shand Kydd

Views of the Hollywood Hills are seen through the living room

O'Neill expanded the outdoor space by adding a hot tub, firepit, BBQ, and outdoor screening room

◄◄

A Bobo Piccoli
for FontanaArte
lamp lights up a
corner of the
primary bedroom.
An artwork by Carl
Hopgood is on
display above the bed

◄

A built-in sofa
by Neutra is
softened with fabrics
from Türkiye by
Robert Allen

WILD, WARM MODERNISM

An aging single-story home on a vast lot offered architect David Thompson and his wife Jamie the perfect expansion for their family of four.

When David Thompson, founder and principal designer of the architecture firm Assembledge+, and Jamie Thompson, a real estate agent, drove onto an 18,000 sq. ft. property for sale, they were instantly entranced by the giant eucalyptus and oak trees that sat canopied over a ranch-style home. The matured woods disappeared into the hillside's darkness that defines Laurel Canyon, a majestic scene that they couldn't let go of. The home itself was fine, minimally dilapidated and a bit "bizarre," but the property and those trees were "just phenomenal – it's like you're in a forest," says David. "It really spoke to us."

Before the couple made any changes, they lived in the house, a practice David advises his clients to do whenever possible. "The experience of living there is a way to learn about the land and the property, how you use it and how it flows," says David. "You learn a lot in that process." David, Jamie, and their two young children spent two years in the home, listening to it, observing the light, and watching the rain fall. The process slowly allowed the home to design itself in a way that best complemented its environmental habitat and the family's own natural movements.

That phenomenal backdrop was also an integral part of the redesign, where they considered and reconsidered schemes that would blur the exterior walls and ceilings, so the landscape could feel one with the interior and vice versa. Apart from the property's raw, captivating beauty, the home and its surroundings had an element of discovery that intrigued David. "I wanted a little bit of that experience to translate in a way," says David, who redesigned the home to reflect a sense of curiosity and intrigue.

With his team at Assembledge+, David came up with a compartmentalized design that hosts three structural volumes, each serving its own purpose. The living, guest, and sleeping pavilions are connected through a datum line that curves and connects the structures together. Floor-to-ceiling glass walls frame the native landscape that folds

Painted cement board and Western red cedar make up the exterior siding ◄

That phenomenal backdrop was also an integral part of the redesign, where they considered and reconsidered schemes that would blur the exterior walls and ceilings, so the landscape could feel one with the interior and vice versa.

→ → A line pendant with midnight globes by Douglas & Bec hangs over the custom table made by Reeve Schley, with a set of 'Metropolitan' chairs by B & B Italia. The painting is by Christina Craemer

into the canyon like a painting. Creatively yet sparingly, the architects brought in a sense of warmth and character to the single-story open floor plan through its slight grade changes, white oak flooring, and exposed ceiling beams – movements that allowed the layout to remain open, yet defined. The couple worked with friend and interior designer Susan Mitnick, who helped fill the home with warm pieces that speak to their aesthetics and personal styles.

The kitchen was designed by Assembledge+ and thoughtfully arranged to eliminate upper cabinetry above the countertops, while still providing ample amounts of storage. David kept the colors dark and muted, so the more innate materials, such as the Calacatta Cremo stone and white oak flooring, could sing.

When it came to the landscape, David and Jamie worked with Fiore Landscape Design to internalize their outdoor rooms. "It's an extension of the living experience into the landscape," says David. They brought in regional drought-resistant botanicals to fill the outdoor space. The couple wanted to introduce a few olive trees to their new home, a species they adored and left at their previous home. They traveled to a nursery and spent the day walking among aging evergreens, finally choosing three eighty-five-year-old olive trees, which had grown together on the lot their entire lives. The trees now sit side by side in their courtyard and are thriving. "They just bring this old, deep soul to the house," says David.

→ A natural flow in and out exists throughout the home. The pool's reflection is seen through the hallway

David and Jamie, with the team at Assembledge+, thoughtfully and successfully assembled all of the city's bests into a work of art the couple now calls home.

Apart from the property's raw, captivating beauty, the home and its surroundings had an element of discovery that intrigued David and Jamie.

The sofas and chairs, from RH, sit over an Abrolhos haute
Bohemian wool rug by Mehraban ➤ ➤

A recessed exhaust fan was installed above the kitchen's
Calacatta Crema marble island ←

In the breakfast nook, Wishbone chairs in steel blue lacquer
surround the 'Saarinen' round dining table by Knoll. The
'Voyage' pendant is by Jens Kajus & Claus Jakobsen ↓

A 'Bolle Sola'
pendant by
Gallotti&Radice
lights the custom
nightstand in the
primary bedroom.
The bed's throw is
by JG Switzer

A casual living room sits off the kitchen and breakfast room and flows into the yard through custom pocket doors

03

BETWEEN THE YEARS

Over the last twenty-three years, Rebecca Rudolph and Colin Thompson have transformed a dilapidated bungalow into a dreamy two-story, three-bedroom home perfect for their family of four.

One step at a time, Rebecca Rudolph and Colin Thompson have creatively reimagined and redesigned their once-dilapidated 500 sq. ft. bungalow into the home of their dreams. Purchased in 2000, the property went through a few versions of itself, the latest being a two-story contemporary home accompanied by a pool and stand-alone studio.

At the time of the home's purchase, Rudolph and Thompson were budding architects, who worked around the home's size and property limitations. Through the home's varying renovations, the couple pulled from their newfound skills, experience, and bookmarked designs to create a space that would comfortably suit and inspire them daily. "Rebecca and I wanted the house to be a reflection of the things we like and how we live," says Thompson, who stepped in as the contractor. He oversaw the construction and added his own time and skill to creatively personalize pockets of the home, like the kitchen island's tiles and dining room's wood walls.

In 2011, Rudolph co-founded the firm Design, Bitches. "D,B combines different types of cultural production within architecture, working across disciplines," shares Rudolph. The home's mixed and mingled designs, like the supermannerist-style graphic Dutch doors between the contemporary floor-to-ceiling windows, reflect Rudolph's interdisciplinary philosophies.

As Rudolph and Thompson continually considered the home's future alongside their own wants and needs, they prioritized spaces and layouts that felt open and receptive to natural light, like they were living in nature. To capture that quintessential indoor-outdoor aspiration, the couple utilized the lot to its entirety, adding additional doors around the home that allowed for an easy flow in and out. They splurged on the floor-to-ceiling glass walls that enclose the downstairs main room, where they watch the family ginkgo shift with seasons, like a majestic painting marking the passing of time.

The upstairs now houses two additional bedrooms, with a non-structural wall between, and each side is currently

The Dutch doors were custom-built by Thompson and painted by Harper Paradowski according to the couple's design

143

Through the home's varying renovations, the couple pulled from their newfound skills, experience, and bookmarked designs to create a space that would comfortably suit and inspire them daily.

occupied by one of their two children. The whole family came together for the design of the upstairs bathroom in choosing colorful accents and patterned tiles that add character and whimsy.

The living room sits next to the kitchen and hosts an array of warm textures and colorful patterns. Records, collectibles, a television, books, artwork, and aging wine all have their story and place in the home. "Everything we do as a family is in this space," says Rudolph.

When it came to the landscape and hardscape, the couple began planting (and replanting) a range of greenery nearly two decades ago. The lush, maturing plants that now shade the yard are a mix of native cacti, aromatics, and herbs, which Rudolph best describes as "little vignettes that evoke different feelings." The pool and deck were recently installed and naturally became the family's favorite spot to cool off and dine – an afternoon the couple could only dream about twenty-three years ago.

→ A pendant by Foscarini floats above the living room's 'Offset' coffee table from Resident. The corner of the Ligne Roset 'Togo' sectional is a coveted spot for movie nights and doubles as a guest bed when needed. A Vitsœ shelving system hosts the family's books and collectibles

The lush, maturing plants that
now shade the yard are a mix
of native cacti, aromatics, and
herbs, which Rudolph best
describes as "little vignettes
that evoke different feelings."

The dining room overlooks the patio that sits
surrounded by lush plants. Encaustic cement tiles by
Huguet line the dining room floor and softly echo the
natural cool hues that surround it. A pendant by
Ravenhill Studio hangs above the table

A custom mattress in Sunbrella fabric cushions the
outdoor daybed that was built by Thompson. The family
sources firewood for the stone firepit from their own lot

A painting of Rudolph's mother and uncle – painted
by her grandfather – hangs on the landing. The soft-
pink wainscoting in the hall is lightly reflected in
the bathroom tiles

A pendant by
Ravenhill Studio
hangs above the
table. The dining
table is by Hay and
the chairs are by
Thonet

The planks and inlays, designed and built by Thompson, were placed at random to poetically mark the heights of their children, along with the likes of André the Giant, Shaq, and an Asian elephant. A Parentesi suspension floor lamp by Achille Castiglioni, Pio Manzù for Flos, brightens the corner, a favorite spot of Thompson's

→

The primary
bedroom, once
painted white, felt
like it was lacking in
some areas, so they
decided to paint it.
The change in color
instantly shifted the
space into the
moody, calm room
they didn't know
they could have.
"We should have
done this a long time
ago," says Rudolph.
"The color affects
the experience
of the space as the
natural light changes
over the course of
the day"

In the upstairs bathroom, a skylight brings in natural light. The vanity is by Ikea and the wall tile is from Daltile

COASTAL CADENCE

A 1930s home nestled in the hills of Silver Lake was reimagined by the new owner and Laun studio to reflect the property's natural rhythm and skyline views.

Friends of friends of friends connected Molly Purnell and Rachel Bullock of Laun studio to musician Drew Straus. Straus had recently purchased a split-level home near Los Angeles's Eastside reservoir and was looking for help with its revival.

Together, they studied the home's potential and focused its architectural redesign in relation to its natural light and skyline views. Straus wanted to introduce warmth and natural materials to the space and often referenced the modernist architecture and aesthetics of Sea Ranch, a coastal community built in the 1960s in Northern California. "Drew is very creative and has a super wide breadth of knowledge about design," says Purnell. White oak floors, Alaskan cedar exterior cladding, hemlock interior ceilings, and a copper roof are a few of the new materials brought in that embody the warmth and serenity Straus desired.

The team also focused on establishing functional, creative spaces for Straus out of the home's existing dark and choppy layout. The upper level's new open layout hosts the bedrooms, kitchen, and living areas, which were thoughtfully zoned by custom millwork and furniture placement. The lower level was converted into a recording studio and office. They also added 500 sq. ft. and an ADU (accessory dwelling unit) off the lower level.

To start, they gutted the home, saving little to nothing of its previous state. "Everything about this house was about the view and lot," remembers Bullock. Next, they removed the dropped ceiling and exposed the beams, bringing light and height to the space. The new loft-like layout allowed for uninterrupted flow between the kitchen, dining nook, and living room. The notion to gently formalize the living and dining room and provide storage sparked the creation of a custom coat closet that doubles as a bookshelf. The bookshelf continues from the front door into the living room, surrounding the fireplace and the door leading to the primary bedroom.

As the team integrated the modern coastal aesthetics that Straus admired into the home, they were careful not to be

Laun and Straus created a bookshelf opposite the closet facing the living room, with clerestory windows floating above. Straus installed preserved driftwood as the closet's door handles. He found the front door on eBay and had it covered in a cobalt-blue high-gloss lacquer

Straus wanted to introduce warmth and natural materials to the space and often referenced the modernist architecture and aesthetics of Sea Ranch, a coastal community built in the 1960s in Northern California.

too serious. "Drew had a vision," remembers Purnell. Playful designs with fluid pops of color, like the driftwood closet handles and a half-moon vintage door sourced from eBay, were brought in by Straus. Straus also displayed an artwork collection inherited from his grandmother around the home. The punch of color in the railings and accents, plus the texture within the rugs and linens, flow from room to room, playing into the whimsy and personality of the home.

The primary bedroom, once two small bedrooms, opens to a modest deck with endless views of the reservoir's hillside. In the connecting bathroom, Straus commissioned artist Sara Bright to paint the shower tiles. Using a sumi ink brush, Bright created a beautiful fluid illustration, pulling from the home's existing blue, yellow, and white palette.

Purnell and Bullock's thoughtful application of purposeful space, natural materials and coastal tones brought an abundance of life to every inch of the home, where Straus can work and retreat among encompassing views and inspiring spaces.

A spectrum of blues and sandy tones fill the home curated by Straus. Following this project, Straus was inspired to start his own design firm, Onsen Studio

157

The punch of color in the railings
and accents, plus the texture
within the rugs and linens, flow
from room to room, playing
into the whimsy and personality
of the home.

Artworks by Sara Bright and Mayumi Oda adorn the
living room walls. The refinished and reupholstered
1970s director chairs sit across from a vintage sofa. A
pendant light from Hay hangs above the coffee table
and Moroccan rug ← ←

The kitchen sink, surrounded by green slate
countertops, overlooks the reservoir. A print by Claes
Oldenburg hangs in the corner ←

An upright piano sits near a selection of inherited and
vintage pieces. The framed prints are by Osborn/Woods ↓

A vintage midcentury table and chairs sit over a Moroccan rug under the hemlock wood ceiling in the dining nook. The home hosts white oak flooring throughout and the exterior is made of Alaskan cedar siding

The aluminum windows were replaced with wood windows, as seen next to the primary bed. A Sol Lewitt poster hangs framed above a vintage credenza

The guest bathroom
is outfitted in teal
glazed tile by Heath
Ceramics and
terracotta flooring
from Zia Tile

The bathroom's new skylights bring in sunlight and views of the home's cypress trees. Straus commissioned local artist Sara Bright to paint over the shower tiles

HILLSIDE DELIGHT

Nestled in the hills of Los Angeles's coveted Eastside neighborhood Echo Park, a century-old home finds a new colorful life.

As the sun sets in Echo Park, its residents retreat into their quiet hillside homes with breathtaking views. When artist Abel Macias found a two-bedroom abode for rent in the desirable neighborhood, he couldn't let it go. The home's Spanish-style architecture, quaint patio, and sweeping views of the city, as well as its proximity to his studio, were just a few of its many attractions. Macias came into the home with a deep respect and admiration for the property and the neighborhood's historical roots. He prioritized revitalizing, instead of renovating, and made minimal changes that creatively responded to the home's lively character but also offered Macias and his partner their own serene escape from the city's hustle.

As Macias settled in, he first took on the dated kitchen, recognizing that the room's prominent feature, the original seafoam linoleum floors, were there to stay. So he expanded its eccentric color onto the kitchen cabinets and window frames, even placing matching teal see-through decals onto the dining room's glass windows. "It gives a shimmery gem-like color. It's really quite beautiful," says Macias. The overgrown patio was also in need of attention and was lightly refreshed so they could host small yet romantic dinner parties with friends. The abundant greenery outside the home's windows and doors is something Macias found soothing; he chose the darkened forest-green hue to reflect that serenity indoors, placing it in the primary bedroom.

Macias begins and ends most days in the living room, where the arched windows offer uninterrupted views of the sun's journey. "Everything revolves around that window. The sun cooks the house at night in the summer and you embrace it in the wintertime," says Macias. A select few of Macias's artworks and objects quietly line the shelves and walls. "Anytime you come home, you have a view and it's a calming space and to clear your mind at the end of the day," says Macias. The century-old casa on the hill now has a new lease on life, and a creative resident who found resourceful ways to sustain its beauty and simplicity.

A few turquoise rocks sit atop the primary bedroom's chest. The wooden masks were picked up at various places from Macias's travels ◄

Macias prioritized revitalizing, instead of renovating, and made minimal changes that creatively responded to the home's lively character but also offered a serene escape from the city's hustle.

An oil painting by Macias, part of the 2019 Terrain Series, hangs above a bookshelf in the main living room. An altar pedestal by Bradley Duncan sits above a Southwest rug ← ←

The small horse painting is by Australian artist Captain Pipe. The sculptural work (right) in the dining room is by Bradley Duncan. An array of pillows, throws, and prints adorn the living room's sofa ←

Donald Judd Writings

A PASSAGE TO INDIA · E. M. Forster

ANNIE LEIBOVITZ AT WORK

Macias begins and ends most days in the living room, where the arched windows offer uninterrupted views of the sun's journey.

A vintage leather arm chair sits under a thriving philodendron plant. The two wooden altar pedestals are by Bradley Duncan and host a few of Macias's keepsakes. Above (and left) of a pedestal is a ceramic work by Alex Reed ◄

A painting (above right) by Jonathan Ryan is hung over a sculptural recycled factory piece that once made balloons. The teal gel window applications adorn the dining room's windows ▼

The framed photo is by Gustavo García-Villa. The Moroccan handmade orb lights the dining room table

The seafoam blue
was extended from
the checkered
flooring to the
kitchen cabinets and
window trim

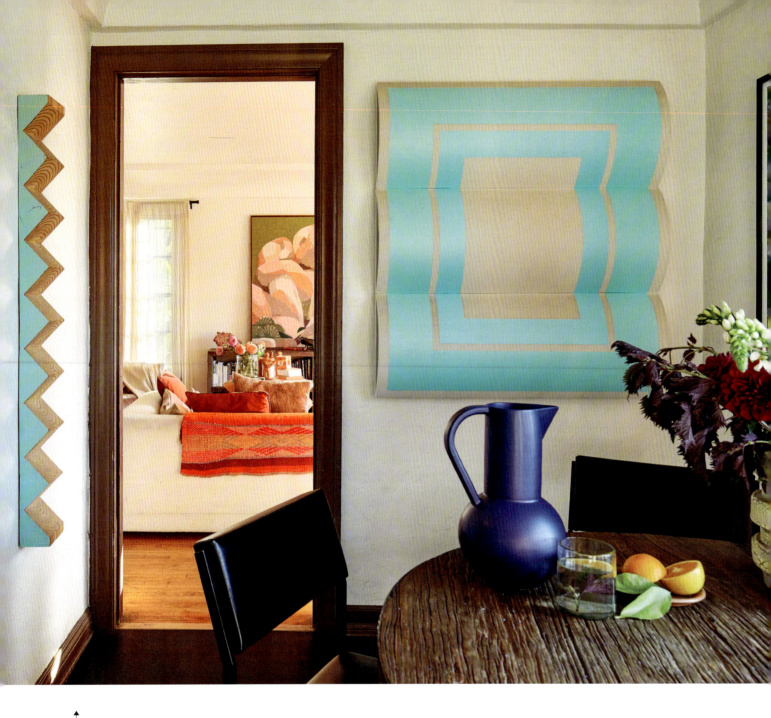

A sculptural work
(left) by Bradley
Duncan hangs in
the dining room,
which connects
the living room to
the kitchen. The
painting (center) is
by Robert Moreland
and the framed
photo (right) by
Gustavo García-Villa

A ceramic work by
Ben Medansky
hangs above the bed
in the primary
bedroom. The table
lamp was picked up
at Lawson-Fenning

RHYTHMIC RENAISSANCE

With the help of Laun Studio, Satya Bhabha's and Carter Batsell's bungalow has undergone a colorfully bold renovation that leaves a lasting impression.

Before Satya Bhabha and Carter Batsell purchased their new home, they brought in Rachel Bullock and Molly Purnell of Laun studio to tour the space. The three walked the property, entertaining the couple's design dreams and the home's potential. Before renovations began, the team agreed to respect the home's original historical character and embrace the property's strengths, including its Downtown views, private landscape, and malleable layout.

A palette of earth-ground hues in soft pink, forest green, and brass were chosen to subtly harmonize the space. Subtleness, however, could not be used to describe the rest of the home. "They are adventurous clients," says Bullock, who took the couple's bold ideas of materials, surfaces, and textures and collaboratively created a striking atmosphere unique to the couple's creative aesthetic while catering to their everyday needs.

Before the couple moved in, the living areas and public spaces were opened up, in a loft-like style, and access to each space was redesigned. "The stairs were terrifying to walk down,"

remembers Bullock, who redesigned the steps with Bhabha entirely, coming up with a natural, more sculptural staircase that artfully bridges the two levels.

They opened the upper level, which consisted of the kitchen, living room, and dining nook. As the floor plan began to form, the couple desired more artistic, customizable solutions to break up the open layout. They worked collaboratively with Bullock and Purnell on a design, sketching ideas and proposing solutions that could also assist with the lack of storage. Ultimately, the architectural cube – a stand-alone, walk-in box placed between the living room and kitchen – was drafted, and the team commissioned Alex Deutschman of Maneuverworks to build it. The multiuse cube, coated in a custom green gloss, serves many functions and simultaneously exists as its own work of art. On the cube's living room side, the recessed shelves that host the couple's art collection were designed by Bhabha. The cube's other sides host a coat closet that opens discreetly behind flush doors, as well as a custom kitchen pantry.

The main living area boasts a variety of textures and finishes. The all-brass cabinetry will patina over time

179

"They are adventurous clients," says Bullock, who took the couple's bold ideas of materials, surfaces, and textures and collaboratively created a striking atmosphere unique to the couple's creative aesthetic while catering to their everyday needs.

The architectural cube is painted in high-gloss custom green lacquer paint. The island is made of pink marble →

In the kitchen, the couple wanted unlacquered brass, knowing the material's finish would patina with age. "It will be an exciting evolution of the house and how it will change," says Purnell.

In the basement below, the darkened ambiance presented quite a contrast to the light-filled upstairs, something they all wanted to lean into. Everyone brought in their ideas to create the perfect, relaxing primary suite for the couple. The moody high-gloss Benjamin Moore paint color on the walls was customized by Laun to complement the House of Hackney wallpaper, chosen by Batsell. Bhabha designed the marble landing step and worked with sculptor G. Ramon Byrne to materialize the drawing. Floor-to-ceiling windows and sliding glass doors were installed on the garden wall opening to the lush, private landscape.

← A pendant by Michael Anastassiades for Flos hangs softly over the LaCividina sofa, while an artwork by Iliodora Margellos graces the wall

The primary bathroom's rose-pink, spa-like walls are coated in finishes that are receptive, yet resilient to water and steam. The room's encompassing nature provides a serene, neutral escape within the colorful quarters it abides in. The home's many layers are filled with poetry, imaginative color, and pockets of surprise, guiding you into unforgettable moments and endless inspiration.

181

A palette of earth-ground hues
in soft pink, forest green, and
brass flows throughout each room,
subtly harmonizing the space.

A vintage chair sourced from Amsterdam Modern sits ← ←
under the sculptural display pockets, designed by Bhabha,
outside of the architectural box. Works by Ben Medansky,
Gabriele Koch, and an LGS Studio planter fill the room

A series of cookbooks fill the shelves of the architectural ←
cube. The flooring is white oak

The primary bedroom's white oak floors were stained, ↓
while custom high-gloss Benjamin Moore paint covers the
walls. The custom green marble receives guests from the
upper level

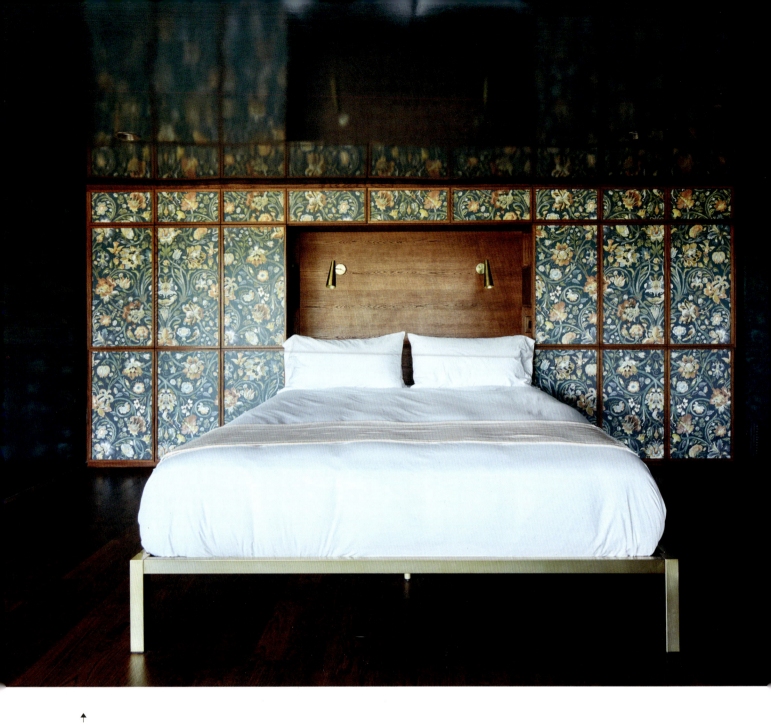

The primary bedroom
was expanded an
additional eight feet
into the garden. The
headboard is clad
in House of Hackney
wallpaper

Plaster walls are
paired with
concrete flooring in
the primary
bathroom. The
room's fixtures are
from California
Faucets and the tub
was sourced from
BainUltra

CALM AND COLLECTED

A rare midcentury gem tucked into the hills of Los Angeles's Eastside neighborhood has been thoughtfully preserved, adored, and cared for by ceramic artist Tracy Wilkinson.

While growing up in England, in a historical melting pot of architecture and interiors, the midcentury-esque Californian lifestyle was always something of a dream to ceramic artist Tracy Wilkinson. Wilkinson adored the American way of life from across the pond before moving to the States nearly thirty years ago, beginning in New York and eventually landing on the West Coast. "I came to California for a job in the 1990s and loved how laid-back it was…and the light. California light is so specific and beautiful," says Wilkinson.

In 2011, Wilkinson dipped back into that midcentury wishful state when she came across a modern hillside home for sale in LA's Eastside neighborhood of Mount Washington, whose "1970s feeling" prompted a visit. Quickly, and in a somewhat serendipitous real estate moment, Wilkinson purchased the property, and come summer she was calling it home.

The original owner's widow passed down the keys, and with them, the home's unique history. The widow's husband worked as a mason and built the entire home from the ground up in 1946. Shortly after its construction, he added additional rooms to accommodate their growing family.

The simple palette of concrete and wood, open layout, abundance of glass, plus its Frank Lloyd Wright-style attributes (whom Wilkinson guesses was a major influence on the owner) illustrate the home's midcentury aesthetics, all attributes that Wilkinson once longingly admired and now preserves.

Wilkinson sparingly made updates and over the last twenty years brought it to a modern-day, livable space. "Houses tell you what they need," says Wilkinson, who cautiously, over time, peeled away bits of the design noise, like the wall-to-wall carpet and aging wood. Paint was used modestly to tone down the varying (and often yellowing) wood grains that were, in some moments, too much. "It needed some simplification to make it more relaxing," says Wilkinson.

The kitchen, which remained intact and untouched by Wilkinson for most of her time in the home, was renovated within the last decade. The hood that hung clunkily over the

Under a paper pendant sits Wilkinson's drafting table ←

→

The kitchen is outfitted in quartz countertops. The stove and oven, which are original to the home, were kept and are in good use to this day. After looking endlessly for new hardware to add into the kitchen cabinets, Wilkinson wasn't satisfied. In the spirit of the home's owner, Wilkinson decided to design and produce the hardware herself

"Houses tell you what they need," says Wilkinson, who cautiously, over time, peeled away bits of the design noise, like the wall-to-wall carpet and aging wood.

island's stove was removed, giving more visual space throughout the room. The kitchen island was extended so guests (and storage) could all find a space.

Wilkinson dressed the living room in soft textures and cool colors that subdue the cement enclave, creating a warm, gentle space with hillside views. The living room's couch, also designed and made by Wilkinson, welcomes guests from the kitchen.

The primary bedroom's white walls and ceilings brighten and enlighten the artist. "I wanted to create a room that had very little detail. A rest for my eyes, something calm and clean," says Wilkinson. The quiet warmth also gives the artist a space to bring in her work, new objects and ideas, testing them within the blank, canvas-like walls.

The terrace's natural extension from the home overlooks the quiet tree line. "It's this little jewel on the top of the hill," she adds. The exterior brickwork has aged to a light pink, a natural evolution that Wilkinson admires. At the end of the day, Wilkinson's favorite spot in the home is next to the fireplace in her beanbag chair, with extra blankets. The perfect 1970s ending in the perfect 1970s home.

←

A framed work by Zoe Crosher hangs in the living room, which features white oak floors. The plates on the coffee table are by Makoto Kagoshima

193

Wilkinson dressed the living room
in soft textures and cool colors
that subdue the cement enclave,
creating a warm, gentle space
with hillside views.

The original owners' foundational brickwork, which
includes inlaid stone screens and patterned cinder bricks,
is sprinkled throughout the home. A glass globe pendant
lights the stairwell →

The living room, kitchen, and dining room have a natural,
open flow that graciously step in and out of one another
and eventually onto the terrace. The ceramic work on the
table is by Kozy Kitchens ←

In the primary bedroom, two of Wilkinson's sculptures sit
above the white credenza ↓

NEUTRA IN SILVER LAKE

Elizabeth Timme and Hank Harris have thoughtfully and cautiously revitalized a Richard Neutra–designed home to best reflect their growing family's needs and the architect's legacy woven within.

Nearly a decade ago, Elizabeth Timme and Hank Harris were living in Beachwood Canyon, scouring the real estate pages for a bigger place while raising their three young children. "We were really struggling to find a home that we could raise them in that had enough bedrooms that was still economic with the uses of space," remembers Timme. The struggle ended when Timme received an email from a friend with a Richard Neutra home for sale in East Los Angeles.

The home, built in 1961, was one of several properties designed by the architect in a localized area of Silver Lake, which is now notably within the Neutra Colony Residential Historic District. The two-story, four-bedroom home had a garage and expansive decks overlooking the reservoir and was being sold by the original Japanese-American family whose parents worked directly with Neutra during its conception. Timme, being a fourth-generation architect, recognized this rarity and went directly to her workshop, where she made a bid-winning Japanese jewelry box with a tiny model of the family's Neutra home inside. Timme and Harris also included a

letter that detailed their values in architecture, stewardship, and family. "I really wanted to raise my kids in a similar culture where we're talking about the value of architecture and its ability to deeply affect people's daily rituals and lives for the better," says Timme. Timme is the founder of Office of Office, an urban planning, design, and architectural practice that specializes in neighborhood-scale community development in Los Angeles and around the country. "How we do that and what that looks like is very inspired by these Neutra homes that were built for the middle class and built for trying to meet people's needs in a way that was dignified and elevating," says Timme.

Neutra and his firm worked directly with the original homeowners to design a house that complemented the couple's specific budget, needs, and wishful add-ons for their growing family – something done with each owner within the Silver Lake Colony that promised a unique yet cohesive modern home for all. Timme and Harris discovered in the archives

A 1970s Mario Lopez Torres 'Palm Tree' light and Sergio Rodrigues–inspired armchair adorn the corner of the living room. The ceramic artwork on the shelf is by Raffi Lehrer ←

The home was one of several properties designed by Richard Neutra in a localized area of Silver Lake, which is now notably within the Neutra Colony Residential Historic District.

correspondence that detailed specific price points for each material and feature, down to the cost of the couple's Knoll dining room chairs. Neutra also excluded options like terrazzo, a pool, or a fireplace and pulled in more of his staple economic materials like linoleum, Formica, and plywood to keep within budget. The final design included Neutra's elegant indoor and outdoor concepts and fluid social spaces, as well as a large driveway for the children to freely play on and customized storage solutions, like the closet's personalized shoe compartments and built-in desks for after-school studies. "This is a real true expression of midcentury architecture," says Timme. "This approach to design was an expression of people's right to space."

The beauty of Neutra's architecture is its ability to carry on its timeless practicality and enlightening features throughout the decades. "There's all these things that are small details that make the home feel really open, like the doors going all the way to the ceiling, but the materiality to which they were built makes it really easy for me to raise a family in," says Timme, who swaps out a damaged linoleum tile or piece

→ A vintage postmodern epoxy and marble coffee table sits between a pair of Sergio Rodrigues–inspired armchairs and a built-in sofa designed by Neutra. Framed prints by Benjamin Critton and Heidi Korsavong hang near the Lightolier sconce, which is original to the home

of the veneer plywood whenever necessary. The layout's clear sightlines from the kitchen through the living spaces have also made socializing during dinner parties and weeknights at home a joy and ease for the family. "There's the level of layering in the space that is really pleasurable to be engaging with people who are guests, family members, or kids because there are all these different ways in which people can use the space and still engage with each other," says Timme. This unique, meaningful piece of architectural history is now in the hands of a thoughtful, creative couple whose values and work within their home and community promise a better future of living for all.

"I really wanted to raise my kids in a similar culture where we're talking about the value of architecture and its ability to deeply affect people's daily rituals and lives for the better," says Timme.

Bend Goods' 'Lucy' chairs in copper are tucked under the kitchen's breakfast table. The oak veneer cabinets surround a Bertazzoni oven ◄◄

The bedroom opens onto a patio with 'Rope' chairs by REI Co-op + West Elm and a Kartell 'Prince Aha' stool →

The dining area features a Lightolier pendant light and a 1936 'Maria' drop-leaf table by Swedish designer Bruno Mathsson. The bench is from Lawson-Fenning and the chairs were designed by Bruno Rey for Dietiker in the 1970s ◄

Timme's father, Bob Timme, made the ladder now standing in the television room. The flooring throughout is made of Forbo linoleum tiles ↓

04

HIGH COLOR

When John and Maria Hill found their dream home, they left everything behind (furniture-wise) and tapped Leah Ring to fill each room with her unique color-blocking palette and vintage finds.

John and Maria Hill were late in the game and only found this perfect midcentury home, built in 1958 on a quiet street, after multiple offers had already been submitted. "Having two growing kids, we were trying to balance something really classic but something that worked really well for our family," says Maria. It's a combo that doesn't seem to stay on the market long, so once they discovered the two-story, 3,300 sq. ft. home with a private yard and pool, they pounced. "Maria and I have always loved midcentury, especially midcentury California homes," says John.

John, a record producer, songwriter, and musician, called in interior designer Leah Ring, of Another Human, whom he had worked with previously on his studio remodel. "I loved working with her," explains John, "and love how she sources vintage things." One of the small but valuable perks of this home was how the previous owners kept the property in near-pristine, midcentury condition, leaving little to be done before moving in. Floor-to-ceiling glass windows, striking structural artistry, and that natural flow indoor and out are a

few notable midcentury moments that abound in this home. "The house is beautiful, so they wanted to be receptive to that," says Ring. As they began the project, they "listened to the house," says Ring, who brought in bold, saturated colors, retro patterns, and vintage pieces in a modern 1960s tone that reflected the home's era, all while keeping the ins and outs of a busy family well into the mix.

Under the living room's white-beam ceiling, clerestory windows bring in ample amounts of West Coast light. The sliding glass doors open to the lush, private courtyard where you can hear the owls at night, if you're lucky. "You feel like you're out of the city," says John. The room's multicolor checkerboard rug anchors the calming, earthy palette that makes up the room and offers a mature, restful respite for family and guests.

Ring webbed practical pieces and fabrics discreetly into the home's layout to accommodate the reality of life's day-to-day. In one memorable instance, Ring helped the owners keep a fun but sensible atmosphere in the family room

A lively mix of pattern and color fill the upstairs family office. "They wanted to keep the shell of the room white with fun saturated colors," says Ring

"Maria and I have always loved midcentury, especially midcentury California homes," says John.

that sits next to the pool – a room that often hosts their guests post-swim – by coating the modular sofa's canvas fabric in cheerful hues of Teflon, a water-repellent finish. As Ring continued the pattern of adding ageless, playful color into every room, she kept the spaces uniquely their own through the use of varying tones, textures, and works of art.

From afternoons by the pool to evenings with records, this house hits all the right notes.

Floor-to-ceiling glass windows, striking structural artistry, and that natural flow indoor and out are a few notable midcentury moments that abound in this home.

A retro-patterned cushion in durable fabric by St. Frank (top) and S. Harris (bottom) adds color and texture to the kitchen's existing millwork corner bench. Artwork by Sarah Faux (left) and Gabrielle Teschner (right) fill the kitchen's walls

A slightly veiled door opens up onto the retro powder room. The floral wallpaper by House of Hackney "echoed its time," says Ring, who paired it with a Gio Ponti F.A. 33 Mirror, a floating countertop, and hints of brass, sparking all the right 1960s feels

The floral rug is
by Rifle Paper Co.

A Vitra Eames side chair is tucked under a muted green desk. Ring chose colors that would mature over time, filling the closet panels with varying subdued tones that create a sense of harmony and intrigue

The primary bed was
designed by Ring
and custom-built by
Arbor Exchange

A Stan Bitters
sculpture (inherited
from the previous
owners) is
permanently installed
in the courtyard, seen
through the primary
bathroom's window.
The Amish stool and
rug are vintage, and
Ring painted the
credenza and updated
the hardware

INTO THE LIGHT

Architects Miguel Ángel Aragonés and Rafael Aragonés took to their Los Angeles property in their famed minimalist fashion, transforming a 1965 home into a dreamy California estate – rooftop garden included.

In 2017, when Miguel Ángel Aragonés and Rafael Aragonés (a father-son architect duo from the Mexico City firm Taller Aragonés, founded by Miguel Aragonés Ángel some forty years ago) acquired a single-story midcentury home on a serene corner in the historic Trousdale Estates neighborhood, they began sketching on day one. They then spent a year in the design phase, waited another year for permits, and spent a final year overseeing its build. Their thoughtful approach to the property's delicate renovation resulted in a 7,000 sq. ft. home that captures it all: natural surroundings, exceptional architecture, and the best of California's light.

Miguel Ángel and Rafael focused first and foremost on the landscape. "It was important to create a refuge surrounded by greenery," says Rafael. As the natural greenery screens grew, a lucid connection to the land and sky was formed, transforming the lot into its own peaceful and private haven.

They then began to work inward, composing artistic architectural structures that would define the home's cohesive,

refined aesthetic. "We designed every single component in the house, so in the end we have a coherent puzzle," says Rafael, who considered the home's entry as its first piece. A customized angular Dutch-style pocket door slides open into the foyer, where a stately recessed oval light (also designed by the architects) radiates a warming glow. "As soon as you arrive to the home, it's serene," says Rafael. "You open the door and time feels slower in that space, in a good way."

As the architects brought in new materials and designs, they thoughtfully approached the delicate balance of preservation and modernization. "When you respect some of the original bones and structures, you have these happy surprises. You encounter certain corners you wouldn't have designed. These sort of interruptions give a little more character to the house," says Rafael. The architects embraced some of the inherited structure, like the living room's chimney, adding to and around the spaces with state-of-the-art appliances, custom furniture, and modern materials. In the kitchen and primary bedroom, the walls were

A geometric pocket door opens into the foyer where a painting by Doug Ohlson greets guests ◄

A mobile piece by
Knopp Ferro is on
display "as a witness
of the air that flows
through the space"
near the living room's
fireplace. The
furniture is from
Poliform while the
rug was custom. The
horse sculpture was
purchased from a
Spanish antique
gallery and dates
back to AD 200   →

"We designed every single component in the house, so in the end we have a coherent puzzle," says Rafael, who considered the home's entry as its first piece.

adorned in a custom elm wood panel – a material chosen for its warmth and versatility. The guest bedrooms were filled with a mix of standard Poliform pieces and the architect's own customized designs, which at times ended as a hybrid between the two. Multifunctional fabricated pieces, like the guest room's closet that transitions into a desk, were creatively interwoven, bringing function and beauty to a new level. "We design piece by piece, space by space, that turns into a whole," says Rafael, who then aesthetically hems it all back in through a unified material palette.

The final, more powerful component to the design's puzzle was color. "When we use color we think of the Mexican tradition of architecture where color is always involved," says Rafael. In and around the delicate white walls, varying intensities of color emanate within site-specific artworks by Regine Schumann and Mercedes Gertz. Paintings by Doug Ohlson, artwork by Heather Hutchison, the central orb within the custom coffee table, and the built-in LED lighting systems bring their own their luminosity and warmth into the space. Come dusk, "the home transforms," says Rafael.

The foyer's fountain
was designed by
Taller Architects and
fabricated by Over
The Top Terrazzo &
Tile Inc., who also
supplied the flooring.
The vertical artwork
(left) is by Regine
Schumann   ←

←

In the primary
bedroom, the elm
wood paneling was
custom-made by
Poliform. The bed,
headboard, and
nightstands are
a blend of custom
and standard
Poliform pieces

→

Terrazzo defines the
primary bathroom's
tub and steps that
lead to the rooftop
garden through its
own private stairwell

In the guest powder
room, a small private
view of the exterior
is seen through the
floor-to-ceiling
windows surrounded
by a privacy wall

SERENE REVERIE

Camilla and Josh Marcus Moak transformed a dreamy hillside home into the perfect creative haven for their young family to adventure into.

A birthday call from a friend led Camilla and Josh Marcus Moak to visit a potential off-market listing on a quiet cul-de-sac in Los Angeles. The midcentury ranch-style home, tucked into a lush canyon on an acre of land, instantly won over the couple. The opportunity came to them in a whirlwind moment of life changes. Camilla and Josh were expecting their second child and had just made the cross-country move to Los Angeles after nearly twenty years in New York. This golden moment to own their first home (with a garden and pool) was not lost on the couple, and they made an offer the next day. "It felt completely kismet," says Camilla.

Camilla, a chef, entrepreneur, and activist, tapped into her years of experience in the restaurant world and in ground-up commercial builds and quickly gathered design ideas, color schemes, and aesthetic goals for the project – often pulling inspiration from the cultural landscapes and spaces of Japan, Italy, and Mexico City. The couple finessed a palette of rustic, romantic neutrals and discovered natural, gregarious materials that would age with ease and grace alongside their growing family. "We really wanted to preserve the house in this beautiful way that it was originally built," says Camilla. They then looked to pare back pieces of the home that felt out of tune. "So much was about subtraction," adds Josh.

As they began to look for a firm to help carry out these ideas, the couple was introduced to Thomas Schneider at Kovac Studio. Camilla was enamored by Kovac Studio's work, and their shared admiration for quality craftsmanship, environmental integrations, and architectural preservation sealed the deal. Schneider suggested Rony Soberanis of Eagle Custom Works as the general contractor, who worked closely with the team to bring the drawings to life in real time. "We all really trusted each other and really envisioned the house in a very similar way," says Camilla.

Everyone worked together to accentuate the natural flow in and out of the home and thoughtfully considered (and reconsidered) every inch of each room into practical, well-designed spaces. "We just wanted to make it

A breakfast and dining nook across from the kitchen features Eames chairs and an Amber Interiors table. On the wall are framed menus that were saved from Camilla's restaurants and the couple's favorites celebrations and other notable moments in time

235

"The whole purpose of the property to me is about balancing and bringing in the outside into the inside and vice versa," says Camilla.

more functional for them and reflect their aesthetic and their style too," says Schneider. Kovac Studio removed the shiny epoxy coating on the cement floors and shuffled in features like the inclusion of skylights and customized closet storage. Camilla found ways to repurpose and reuse wherever possible; for example, the kitchen's pendant once hung in Camilla's New York restaurant, bricks found around the property now frame the garden beds, and a well-traveled credenza was converted into the primary bathroom's vanity (with a new custom stone basin affixed on top).

When it came to the kitchen and its somewhat unforgiving layout, the delicate pairing of function and aesthetics was a creative challenge that Camilla and Kovac Studio orchestrated elegantly. "I look at limitations as sparks for creativity," says Camilla. To maximize storage and accommodate easier paths, a customized island was added, hardware was excluded from the cabinets, and the touchless appliances by Miele (who Camilla partnered with) fit in like a glove. "Every inch counted in that kitchen," remembers Schneider. "And it's great."

The rest of the home hosts a mix of vintage furniture and designer pieces that fold in nicely with other high-performance pieces and fabrics, like the Armadillo carpets, an everyday 'Cloud' couch covered in machine-washable material, Workstead lighting, and a Noguchi pendant, to name a few. Textures were brought in to add warmth and variety into the neutral palette and were considered a "proxy for color," Josh noted. The bathrooms were sealed in a waterproof Meoded finish and outfitted in soothing hues and pleasant fixtures.

As the home extends naturally into a vast, private lawn, a chicken coop, a pool, a media room, and multiple gardens await.

The kitchen's Empire Grey limestone countertop is matched with vintage Cleo Baldon for Terra Furniture barstools, covered in machine-washable fabric. The range is by Miele and the vent is covered in Portola Roman Clay in a custom color. The floating silver maple wood shelves were repurposed from Camilla's former restaurant

236

An Isamu Noguchi pendant hangs over the 'Diptiq' tables by
Christian Woo. The 'Cloud' sofa by Restoration Hardware borders
the Armadillo rug. A Harland Miller print from White Cube hangs
above a restored vintage Jesse French & Sons piano

In the children's bedroom, a pair of cribs by Crate & Kids sit on
a vintage rug, while Heidi Merrick surfboards are fastened to the
wall. The light fixture is by Allied Maker

The primary
bedroom's side table
is by Isaac
Friedman-Heiman
for Souda, and the
light fixture is by
Workstead. The bed
frame was found at
Croft House

The soaking tub is
from Zen Bathworks,
with faucets from
California Faucets.
The paint is Portola
Roman Clay in a
custom color.
The pendant is
Nickey Kehoe

COAST TO COAST

A creative director, a fashion entrepreneur, and an interior architect came together to blend their own contemporary styles and cultural makeup into a two-story home that hadn't been updated in a hundred years.

"It's always been my dream to live in this neighborhood," says Aimee Song, a fashion entrepreneur whose family used to drive from their apartment in Downtown Los Angeles to the idyllic tree-lined street each holiday to trick-or-treat and peruse its festive decorations. Several years ago, Song's childhood wishes came true when she moved into her first home, a small fixer-upper in her idolized neighborhood. This was it, she thought, until a few years later she walked by yet another fixer-upper that was on a slightly better street with a slightly bigger yard (and pool) – something she couldn't let pass her by. So Song and her partner Jacopo Moschin, a creative director, made the switch. Their new Spanish-style home, built in the early part of the twentieth century, was beautiful and captivating, but a bit dated. "Once we saw past the 'oldness' of the house, we fell in love with all of the original arches and beautiful doors," says Song.

Before moving in, the couple called upon Moschin's childhood friend, the interior architect and designer Antonio Forteleoni, to help with its revival. Moschin and Forteleoni are both from Italy and had worked together previously on Moschin's Milan apartment. For this project, they delicately considered how everyone's personal aesthetics and furniture (such as the George Nakashima chairs and nineteenth-century Chinese bench) would co-exist within a space that they wanted to cohesively feel raw, gentle, and beautiful. Italy's rugged coastline was a point of reference and inspiration for the redesign. "We wanted to keep that Mediterranean soul, but make it modern," says Forteleoni. Song and Moschin also referenced their travels to Antwerp and contemporary buildings by Axel Vervoordt and Vincent Van Duysen, which also became a pocket reference during the design phase. That eclectic mesh of styles, influence, designer pieces, and wishful aesthetics was then brought to life (all in consideration of the home's original style) and completed one room at a time.

In the living room, Forteleoni designed a fireplace cut from one large, partly unfinished block of travertine that perfectly captures the home's aesthetic. The rock's exposed,

The framed print *Kristen 1996*, by Inez & Vinoodh, was purchased from Matthew Marks Gallery. The chair is from De La Espada

The soft, delicate textures found within the room's curation of vintage pieces and works of art offer that sought-after coastal tranquility.

rugged edges gracefully transition into a polished square frame that surrounds the firebox. "The result is unique, raw, yet very refined," adds Song. The soft, delicate textures found within the room's curation of vintage pieces and works of art also offer that sought-after coastal tranquility. And the kitchen and primary bathroom's variegated marble, wooden walnut cabinets, and travertine floors continue to parallel the ageless beauty that reflects the striking shorelines bordering Italy and California's coastlines.

As the project unfolded, Forteleoni noticed and embraced the social (and in return architectural) differences of these two coasts. He then hemmed in their subtle polarities within the design schemes whenever possible. For example, in the kitchen, he opened up the space under the countertop so guests could easily pull up a chair and be part of the conversation at any angle and any edge. This small but notable design concept gives in to the European way of congregating around a kitchen, where everyone comes together and has an open seat at the most important moment of the day: mealtime. "It is the most used space and the heart of the house," adds Song. And when it comes to the West Coast way of life, "of course we made it very Californian, in the way of that being very big walk-in closets," says Forteleoni, who converted a sixth bedroom into a walk-in closet for Song and Moschin and opened up the lower-level social spaces so they flow in and out of the backyard – a West Coast necessity. That expanded use of space and the comfort it embodies is something Forteleoni says he's now bringing into his European projects.

Forteleoni, Moschin, and Song's beautiful collaboration of backgrounds, expertise, and practical must-haves was cautiously and creatively placed within a century-old home that speaks to each creative's personal ambitions, something they can all raise a glass to – *Saluti!*

→ In the dining room, the elegant 'En Forme Libre' table, by Charlotte Perriand from Cassina, is surrounded by original nineteenth-century George Nakashima chairs. The mauve rug is from Armadillo. The black cabinet is from Korea and dates back to the 1800s. The ceramic vase was designed by Moschin and fired by Chie Fujii

"We wanted to keep that Mediterranean soul, but make it modern," says Forteleoni.

← Song's vintage Mario Bellini 'Camaleonda' sofa (purchased from Morentz) sits across from the travertine fireplace custom-designed by Forteleoni. The marble table behind the sofa was designed by Song. Above the table, a ceramic vase by Philip M. Soucy is on display. An olive tree grabs light from the room's corner windows

→ Calacatta Viola marble has been used for the kitchen's island, backsplash, and countertops. The custom wood cabinetry was designed by Forteleoni and made of walnut. The faucets are by Brizo

↓ The breakfast room's table is from RH and the chairs are by De La Espada. The bench is from Olive Ateliers and the glazed Chinese vases are from Berbere Imports

A twentieth-century Indonesian dish from Timor Island is on display above the Senufo coffee table. The vintage midcentury 'Chandigarh' chair was designed by Pierre Jeanneret. The artwork is by Japanese artist Kiyoshi Nakagami

The classic 'Barcelona' leather daybed, designed by Ludwig Mies van der Rohe and produced by Knoll, and the Charlotte Perriand chair, made by Cassina, are both from Design Within Reach. The custom walnut library keeps the couple's literary keepsakes. On the shelf is an unframed, unfinished portrait of the French novelist George Sand, circa 1800

↑

The wooden
nightstands are from
the Rose Bowl Flea
Market. The rug is by
Armadillo and the
artwork was gifted
from Japanese artist
Kiyoshi Nakagami

In the primary
bathroom, the
soothing palette of
marble and walnut
continues. The sink
is made of Cipollino
marble and the
shower of travertine.
An original
nineteenth-century
George Nakashima
chair sits in the
corner. The faucets
are by Brizo

CREDITS

SEA OF CHANGE
PP. 10—23
Owner: Elizabeth Paige Smith and
Christopher Stringer
elizabethpaigesmith.com
Syng.io
Photography by Ye Rin Mok
yerinmok.com
@yerinmok

**CLASSICALLY
ONE-OF-A-KIND**
PP. 24—35
Owner: Meredith Chin
Interior Design: Mat Sanders
Photography by Ye Rin Mok
yerinmok.com
@yerinmok

NEW ENDEAVORS
PP. 6, 8, & 36—47
Owner: Sandrine Abessera
and Lubov Azria
Architect: Kurt Simon
Interior Design: Gabriella Kuti
www.atraform.com
@Gabriella____Kuti
Photography by Ye Rin Mok
yerinmok.com
@yerinmok

ODE TO THE PAST
PP. 48—59
Owner: Kate Brien Kitz and David Kitz
Architect: Andrew Hall, Aha Design
aha-arc.com
@ahaandd
Interior Decorator: Lafayette Studio
lafayette-studio.com
@lafayette__studio
Landscape Designers: Molly Funk,
Mary Lange, and Donielle Kaufman
Stylist: Kate Brien Kitz
Photography by Tim Hirschmann
timhirschmann.com
@timhirschmann

CALIFORNIA DREAM
PP. 60 & 62—73
Owner: Sophie Lawrence Parker &
Kevin Parker
@solaw
Interior Design: Jaime Lee Major,
MAJOR Spaces
@majorspaces
major-spaces.com
Photography by Ye Rin Mok
yerinmok.com
@yerinmok

FOREVER HOLLYWOOD
PP. 74—83
Resident: Kimberly Biehl Boaz
and Greg Boaz
Interior Decorator: Kimberly Biehl
Photography by Tim Hirschmann
timhirschmann.com
@timhirschmann

BALANCING ACT
PP. 84—95
Owner: Rosa Park & Rich Stapleton
@rosaliapark
Photography by Ye Rin Mok
yerinmok.com
@yerinmok

LACONIC GRANDEUR
PP. 96—107
Owner: David Alhadeff
and Jason Duzansky
thefutureperfect.com
@thefutureperfect
@davidalhadeff
Architect: Arthur S. Heineman
Landscape Design: Studio Art Luna
artlunastudio.com
@art__luna
Photography by Tim Hirschmann
timhirschmann.com
@timhirschmann

LAYERED ELEGANCE
PP. 108—117
Owner: Annie Potts and James
Hayman
Photography by Tim Hirschmann
timhirschmann.com
@timhirschmann

THE HAILEY HOUSE
PP. 118—127
Owner: Patrick Thomas O'Neill
Architect: Richard Neutra
Interior Design: Anthony Barsoumian
Project Designer, Manager:
Dr. Barbara Lamprecht
barbaralamprecht.com
Photography by Tim Hirschmann
timhirschmann.com
@timhirschmann

WILD, WARM MODERNISM
PP. 128—139
Owner: David and Jamie Thompson
Architect: David Thompson, AIA,
Assembledge+
assembledge.com
@assembledge
Interior Decorator: Susan Mitnick
www.susanmitnick.com
@susanmitnickdesignstudio
Stylist: Lisa Rowe
@rowelosangeles
Photography by Tim Hirschmann
timhirschmann.com
@timhirschmann

BETWEEN THE YEARS
PP. 142—153
Owners/Architects: Rebecca Rudolph
(of Design, Bitches)
and Colin Thompson
@design_bitches
Photography by Tim Hirschmann
timhirschmann.com
@timhirschmann

COASTAL CADENCE
PP. 154—165
Owner: Drew Straus
Architect: Laun Studio
launlosangeles.com
@launlosangeles
Interior Design: Onsen Studio
onsenstudio.com
@_onsen_
Photography by Ye Rin Mok
yerinmok.com
@yerinmok

HILLSIDE DELIGHT
PP. 166—177
Resident: Abel Macias
@abelmac
Stylist: Tomas DeLucia
tomas-delucia.com
Photography by Ye Rin Mok
yerinmok.com
@yerinmok

RHYTHMIC RENAISSANCE
PP. 140 & 178—189
Owner: Carter Batsell
and Satya Bhabha
Architect: Laun Studio
launlosangeles.com
@launlosangeles
Photography by Ye Rin Mok
yerinmok.com
@yerinmok

CALM AND COLLECTED
PP. 190—199
Owner: Tracy Wilkinson
Photography by Tim Hirschmann
timhirschmann.com
@timhirschmann

NEUTRA IN SILVER LAKE
PP. 200—209
Owner: Elizabeth Timme
and Hank Harris
Architect: Richard Neutra
Stylist: Claire Walsh
Photography by Tim Hirschmann
timhirschmann.com
@timhirschmann

HIGH COLOR
PP. 212—223
Owner: John Hill and Maria Hill
Interior Design: Another Human
anotherhuman.la
@anotherhumandesign
Photography by Ye Rin Mok
yerinmok.com
@yerinmok

INTO THE LIGHT
PP. 210 & 224—233
Owner: Miguel Ángel Aragonés and
Rafael Aragonés
Architect: Taller Aragonés
talleraragones.com.mx
Photography by Tim Hirschmann
timhirschmann.com
@timhirschmann

SERENE REVERIE
PP. 234—241
Owner: Camilla and Josh Marcus Moak
Architect: Kovac Studio
@kovacstudio
www.kovac.studio.com
Design: Camilla Marcus
@camilla.marcus
Stylist: Lisa Rowe
@rowelosangeles
Photography by Tim Hirschmann
timhirschmann.com
@timhirschmann

COAST TO COAST
PP. 242—253
Owner: Aimee Song
and Jacopo Moschin
Interior Architect & Designer:
Antonio Forteleoni
www.forteleoni.studio
@aforteleoni
Florals: Sean Shakes
Stylist: Jacopo Moschin
and Antonio Forteleoni
Photography by Ye Rin Mok
yerinmok.com
@yerinmok

Texts: Corynne W. Pless, @corynnestudio, corynnewarepless.com
Photography: Tim Hirschmann & Ye Rin Mok
Design: Carolina Amell
Editing: Léa Teuscher

Front cover image:
Owner: Sophie Lawrence Parker & Kevin Parker @solaw
Interior Design: Jaime Lee Major, MAJOR Spaces, @majorspaces, major-spaces.com
Photography by Ye Rin Mok, yerinmok.com, @yerinmok

Sign up for our newsletter with news about new and forthcoming publications on art, interior design, food & travel, photography and fashion as well as exclusive offers and events. If you have any questions or comments about the material in this book, please do not hesitate to contact our editorial team: art@lannoo.com

©Lannoo Publishers, Belgium, 2023
D/2024/45/133– NUR 450/454
ISBN 978-94-014-9047-4
www.lannoo.com